CONCILIUM

Religion in the Eighties

CONCILIUM

Concilium 195 (1/1988): Ecumenism

CONCILIUM

List of Members
Advisory Committee: Ecumenism

A COUNCIL
FOR
PEACE

Edited by
Hans Küng
and
Jürgen Moltmann

English Language Editor
James Aitken Gardiner

T. & T. CLARK LTD
Edinburgh

February 1988
T. & T. Clark Ltd, 59 George Street, Edinburgh EH2 2LQ
ISBN: 0 567 30075 7

ISSN: 0010-5236

Typeset by C. R. Barber & Partners (Highlands) Ltd, Fort William
Printed by Page Brothers (Norwich) Ltd

Concilium: Published February, April, June, August, October, December.
Subscriptions 1988: UK: £27.50 (including postage and packing); USA: US$49.95 (including air mail postage and packing); Canada: Canadian$59.95 (including air mail postage and packing); other countries: £27.50 (including postage and packing).

CONTENTS

Concilium 195 Special Column

A COUNCIL FOR PEACE

Part I
Peace in Face of the Nuclear Holocaust

CONCILIUM 195 Special Column

Gregory Baum

Mary of the Magnificat

THE VENERATION of the Blessed Virgin Mary is deeply rooted in the Catholic tradition. Catholics have always loved Our Lady. It is therefore a puzzling phenomenon that after Vatican Council II devotion to Mary visibly declined. This sudden lessening of interest demands explanation. Even the Marian Year which started on 7 June 1987, though strongly recommended by Pope John Paul's encyclical Redemptoris Mater, does not seem to have much influence on the piety of Catholics in North America. Even among the people of Quebec, heirs of a traditional Catholic culture, the decline in Marian devotion is quite marked. According to reports, the European Catholic experience is similar. This development calls for historical explanation.

The Vatican Council produced an important text on the Blessed Virgin Mary (Lumen gentium, ch. 8) that presented the mother of Jesus as an integral part of the redemptive mystery of the Church. This text might well have stirred Catholic people to greater devotion. But that did not take place. Why not?

Some critics have suggested that the new openness to the world introduced by Vatican II led to a certain secularisation among Catholics and that for this reason Marian devotion and the veneration of the saints have suffered a decline. Catholics who accept this explanation can easily make devotion to Mary and the cult of her apparitions into a public gesture expressing resistance to the spirit of Vatican II.

It is, of course, quite true that in the developed countries of the West a certain secularisation of culture had been taking place for a long time. Vatican II tried to find a creative response to this trend, and the conciliar renewal in fact heightened certain religious practices in the Catholic

Church. Thanks to a more participatory liturgy and a better understanding of sin and forgiveness, Catholics have learnt to receive holy communion every time they attend Mass. The most visible change in post-Vatican II parish life is the presence of the whole congregation at the Lord's table.

Why, then, the decline of Marian piety? In my opinion Vatican II does have something to do with it. For one thing, the Council put an exceptionally strong emphasis on Holy Scripture as source of revelation, basis of catechetics, focus of preaching, soul of theology, and guide to the spiritual life. The liturgy now makes the Biblical texts available and interprets them to the people, and in so doing the liturgy itself has become more, conformed to the simplicities of the Bible. In parts of the Church located in highly literate cultures, where reading and writing dominate the imagination, Catholics have become a biblical people. They now hear God's Word addressed to them, they have new religious experiences, they are confirmed, judged, forgiven and consoled by the Book that is handed them by the Church. Catholics are led to a spirituality markedly different from the pious imagination created by the veneration of our Lady and devotion to the saints in the traditional forms.

Secondly, the Vatican Council has generated a scriptural spirituality, mediated by liturgy, that is oriented towards engagement in the world. Catholics now possess a stronger sense of mission. People long to encounter God in meeting with and listening to others, and—more than that—in bearing the burden with others and struggling with them for social justice. The God who speaks to them in Scripture also addresses them through the important experiences they have in the world. Discipleship of Jesus has acquired a this-worldly orientation. Contemplation no longer excludes the others, instead it embraces them, especially the oppressed others. Again, this spirituality is in contrast with the other-worldly spirit of inherited Marian devotions.

In my opinion it is this twofold transformation of Catholic spirituality that explains the relative indifference of Catholics toward the veneration of Mary.

Perhaps one should add that many Catholic women are also unhappy that the Church continues to present Mary as model to them. Mary's life as a woman was defined by a culture very different from our own. Contemporary women want to imitate Mary formaliter—*by growing in faith, hope and love; but they do not want to imitate her* materialiter—*by copying her role in society as helper and servant.*

At the same time I do not believe for one moment that devotion to Mary will fade away and disappear from Roman Catholicism. In the spiritual universe created by Vatican II we will see appear new forms of Marian devotion and new attention to the saints. In certain parts, such as Latin America, the veneration of Mary creates a certain continuity with an ancient religious culture that nourishes the imagination of the people and constitutes their identity. The struggle for social justice in these and all parts of the world has created among Catholics a special attachment to Mary of the Magnificat, who praises God for the redemption-and-liberation ushered in by her son, Jesus. The solidarity Catholics extend to the poor and oppressed among the living also embraces the little people and the witnesses who have died and gone before them. Solidarity unites Catholics with the communion of saints.

Confronting the crimes of oppression and the immense human suffering taking place in this century, Christians have had to be very serious. As we move toward nuclear conflict in one part of the world and mass starvation in another, Christians find it increasingly difficult to dance and to laugh. Is it still responsible to enjoy the beauty of the cosmos and find happiness in human tenderness? Or must this be left to the hard-hearted who shrug off the cries of the innocent? Catholics find in Mary an answer to this question. She invites us to interrupt the serious mood and celebrate the beauty of creation, to dance and to laugh, to reassure us of our destiny as human beings and strengthen us for the time of trial.

Note that this Special Column, like others in this series, is written under the sole responsibility of the author.

A COUNCIL FOR PEACE

Editorial
An Ecumenical Assembly for Peace

THE DEMAND for a large ecumenical gathering where all Christianity on earth will unanimously affirm God's peace for this mortally threatened world, is not new. It was Dietrich Bonhoeffer who, in 1934 at the general meeting of the world federation for international work towards friendship between churches and of the ecumenical council for practical Christianity, made the following demand: 'Only the one great ecumenical council of Christ's holy Church from all corners of the earth can say it in such a way that the world, gnashing its teeth, must hear the word of peace, and that the peoples of the world will rejoice because Christ's Church takes the weapons from its sons' hands in the name of Christ and forbids them war and proclaims peace across the whole mad world' (cf. N. Greinacher on this in *Concilium* 190 (2/1987, p. xi). That was said before the Second World War, before Auschwitz and before Hiroshima. Since Hiroshima and 1945 we have entered a new world situation. We exist in the secular 'end-time', i.e. in the time in which the nuclear end of mankind is possible at any moment (G. Anders). Because people cannot forget what they know and cannot become incapable of doing what they can now do, the nuclear age is the last age of mankind. We must live and make time for living under the nuclear threat. Mankind has become mortal (M. Gorbachev). Its survival lies in its own hands.

With this issue of *Concilium* we would like to prepare the way for the necessary 'Ecumenical Assembly for Peace': 'Time is pressing'. (C. Fr. v. Weizsäcker). The Christian churches must together affirm that they commit themselves passionately, with one voice and with all their strength, to finding a way out of the three crises threatening mankind: the East-West conflict, the North-South conflict and the ecological crisis; and that they are making a stand for a new culture of justice, peace and the preservation of creation. But it is not only a question of this practical goal, but also of Church and theology at last becoming aware of the new world situation and of developing their own answers to these challenges.

We have conceived this issue so that after the theses of Carl Friedrich von Weizsäcker a report by Lukas Fischer brings us up to date with ecumenical discussion and preparation of the 'Assembly for Peace'. In Part I Rosemary Ruether, Metropolitan Damaskinos, Wolfgang Huber, Stanley Hauerwas and Dietmar Mieth then tell us about the peace documents from the Christian churches, about 'War and Peace' in the Christian tradition and according to Christ's Sermon on the Mount. These show clearly how the still divided Christian churches have today already reached converging answers in this vital human matter. Consequently it is perfectly possible that the churches will be speaking at the 'Assembly for Peace' with one voice and in totally concrete terms.

Part II takes up the cry for justice in face of the mass misery in the Third World. There will be no peace in the world without justice. Justice not 'security' creates peace. That was why in 1983 in Vancouver 'justice' was put at the top of the agenda. Jon Sobrino, with regard to the 'Third World' in Latin America, and Hans Diefenbacher, with regard to the 'Third World' in Europe, show how a high level of armaments produces poverty there as well as here. Enda McDonagh from Ireland and Ignacio Ellacuria from Latin America report on meaningful ways of resisting threat and impoverishment.

In Part III we direct attention to problem areas to give impetus to 'new thinking' in the nuclear age. Clarke Chapman takes a critical look at the 'Armageddon theology' of the political exponents of the Apocalypse Theory in the USA. Joachim Garstecki describes the main features of the 'new thinking' with which Mikhail Gorbachev has replaced the old Marxist doctrine of the war that is just because it is necessary. Finally Anne Carr confronts churches and Christians with the question of conscience, namely if and how far they are capable of peace. Jürgen Moltmann's concluding contribution is intended to stress what the churches as churches of Christ, and what theology as Christian theology, have to say today about justice and peace.

Hans Küng
Jürgen Moltmann

Translated by Gordon Wood

INTRODUCTION

Carl Friedrich von Weizsäcker

Time is pressing. A world assembly of Christians for justice, peace and the preservation of creation.

Theses

I. Title and subject matter

1. A world assembly of Christians for *justice, peace* and *the preservation of creation* should be convened.
2. Mankind is today in a crisis whose catastrophic climax probably still lies ahead of us. Resolute action is therefore necessary.
3. The crisis can be seen in the three areas of justice, peace and nature. Attitudes in these areas can be challenged in a way that is both open to an ethical concensus and realisable in political terms.
4. With regard to these three areas, *unity among Christians and agreement among world religions* is possible and imperative. A world-wide politically effective system of laws must be demanded.

II. Justice

1. No peace without justice, no justice without peace.
    No justice without freedom, no freedom without justice.
2. Justice means both *legality*, i.e., national and international law including human rights, and also *social justice*, without which the poor derive no benefit from their legal rights.
3. The assembly should be willing to make and must make concrete statements on topics such as racism, women's rights, the use of force and unemployment.

3

4.   A system of ethics common to all Christians is possible. An achievable world-wide economic system is politically necessary.

III. Peace

1.   The time has come when the political institution of war *must* and *can* be overcome.
2.   The danger of a third world war has not been exorcised. Nuclear deterrence has granted us a breathing space. It is morally questionable and offers no permanent certainty. It has not prevented more than a hundred non-nuclear wars since 1945. Peace can be permanently secured only on a political and not on a technological basis.
3.   The assembly must, if it can do so in time, urgently demand of the great powers a common policy of détente, arms reduction, economic and cultural co-operation.
4.   A common Christian theology of peace will be possible for the first time for 1700 years. To overcome war as an institution means, in political terms, that *states must give up their sovereign right* to wage war.

IV. Creation

1.   No peace among mankind without *peace with nature*. No peace with nature without peace among mankind.
2.   It is non-technological behaviour to achieve everything that is technologically possible. Today we are in danger of destroying the basis of the existence of plants, animals and people in the course of a few decades.
3.   The assembly will have to involve itself in questions concerning the politics of international energy, agriculture, the protection of forests, particularly in the tropics.
4.   A science which considers itself not responsible for its consequences, and a technology which is not consciously planned to take account of error, are morally and politically immature. The great environmental problems must be dealt with within the framework of a world-wide economic system.

Translated by Gordon Wood

Lukas Vischer

Ecumenical Preparations for a World Peace Assembly

DURING THE last few years the call for a world assembly of the churches has sounded with increasing insistence. In view of the dangers that threaten us, is it not the churches' inescapable duty to make an unequivocal witness for peace? Should not the churches be able to unite across confessional, national and political or social barriers and speak with one voice? No doubt even the united voice of such a 'council' might go unremarked. But does not the churches' Lord require them to testify clearly to the whole world that the gospel of Jesus Christ has opened a different way from the way of self-destruction?

A start was made by the call issued by the *World Alliance of Reformed Churches* immediately after its general assembly held in Ottawa in 1982. The executive committee of the World Alliance sent out an appeal to its member churches to 'stand together and renew their commitment to *peace and justice*'. The committee also proposed that 'all the churches which acknowledge Jesus as Lord and Saviour should form an alliance for *peace and justice*'. 'Even if they still hold differing opinions on many subjects ... yet in today's world they are faced with the same challenges in relation to peace and justice ... in order to give this alliance visible expression, we suggest that the World Council of Churches should make preparations for a world assembly in which all the churches would take part and render a common witness on ways to *peace and justice*, and that this assembly should be convened as soon as possible.' Representatives of the evangelical churches in the German Democratic Republic made similar proposals at about the same time. At its plenary meeting in Vancouver the World Council of Churches took up these

5

suggestions and called upon the churches 'to engage in a conciliar process of mutual commitment (alliance) to *justice, peace and the preservation of the creation*'. It expressly stated that the programmes of the World Council of Churches should be directed towards bringing this programme to fruition. Some two years later, further action was taken. The Conference of the German Evangelical Church held in Dusseldorf issued a clarion call to the churches to convene a 'Council of peace'. The text drawn up by Carl Friedrich von Weiszäcker contained the words: 'Peace is now a condition of the survival of mankind. Peace is not assured. At an ecumenical council called for the sake of peace, the churches must together take responsibility for speaking a word that the world cannot ignore. Time is running out ...' This text received the support of the *Lutheran World Federation*. The executive committee instructed its General Secretary to work together with the Roman Catholic church, the world-wide Christian communions, the World Council of Churches and other ecclesiastical international organisations and their administrations in the planning of such a meeting. 'This meeting should promote a stronger commitment to peace within the Christian community. Teaching about the "just war" should be replaced by teaching about the *just peace*. Its aim must be to overcome the manufacture of atomic weapons and the threat of their development and use ... this teaching should also lay stress on the intimate connection between peace, justice and the preservation of the creation.' (Declaration of July 1986). The *World Alliance of Reformed Churches* also reverted to its proposal in an open letter to the World Council of Churches and pressed for the speedy convening of a 'world assembly for justice, peace and the preservation of the creation'. It emphasised that this should not be just a *meeting of 'leaders'* but that it should grow out of a 'conciliar process'. This call for a world assembly was heard not only from the large organisations but also from individual churches, movements and groups, predominantly in Europe and North America. For its part, the Roman Catholic church also took a similar initiative. In October 1986 *Pope John Paul II* invited representatives both of the churches and of other religions to Assisi for a day of prayer for peace, and in this way a community of prayer such as the world had scarcely seen before came into being.

Under the stimulus of these appeals and initiatives, the World Council of Churches again became active. In November 1986 it organised an international consultation in order to test the prospects for a world assembly. Then in January 1987 the Central Committee of the World Council of Churches resolved to convene a world assembly for justice, peace and the preservation of the creation for the summer of 1990. It issued an urgent call to the Roman Catholic church to take part in this meeting. At the same time it clearly stated that a world assembly could only speak an effective word if preparations had been made for it by regional assemblies in the various continents. In March 1987 the Conference of European Churches decided to hold a regional conference of this kind in 1989. Its theme will be 'Peace with Justice'. Other ecclesiastical organisations are expected to take similar action.

AN ANCIENT HOPE REVIVED

The proposal for a world assembly of all the churches is not new. In particular, it has very deep roots in the more recent manifestations of the ecumenical movement. Repeated appeals have been made to the churches to embark upon the venture of a conciliar meeting, and in this way not only to rediscover their unity but also to give a more effective testimony to the world. One example of this was the appeal issued by the Reformed theologian Philip Schaff (1819–93). Although Schaff was Swiss by birth, he lived and worked in the United States. Both in his theological work and in the course of numerous journeys he worked indefatigably for the rapprochement and unity of the separated churches. He was one of the leading pioneers both of the *Evangelical Alliance* and of the *World Federation of Reformed Churches*. Shortly before his death he issued a call for a council of the churches, at the World Congress of Religions which was held in connection with the World Exhibition in Chicago. 'What would happen to us if the Pope, in the spirit of Gregory I, and moved by a higher authority, unerringly declared his fallibility in all matters lying outside his own communion and invited the Orthodox and the Protestants to a fraternal pan-Christian council to be held in Jerusalem, the city in which the mother church of all Christendom held the first council of reconciliation and peace! But whether in Jerusalem or at Rome, in Berlin or on the shores of the Mississippi, the war between Rome and Constantinople and that between Rome, Wittenberg, Geneva and Oxford will be fought to a peaceful conclusion as soon as the churches are christianised to the depths, and the Christian confessions have come together in the one confession of Christ.' (See David S. Schaff, *The Life of Philip Schaff*, New York 1897, p. 488).

And how easily could this vision of a world assembly of all churches be combined with the aim of making a common witness to peace! From its earliest beginnings the ecumenical movement has been characterised by commitment to peace. Indeed, many have found their motivation for seeking co-operation with churches of other confessions only in the task of seeking to counter the menace of war. Ever since its beginnings many people have looked upon the ecumenical movement as a peace movement. We have only to think of the efforts made by some of the evangelical churches in the years immediately preceding the First World War to convene *a peace conference*.

Alas, when they eventually did get together it was already too late. The representatives who met in Constance were overtaken by the outbreak of war. Some of the participants went to London, where they founded the 'World Alliance for Peace through the Churches' before separating, and this was one of the movements that paved the way for the formation of the World Council of Churches. Then there were the repeated efforts made during the First World War to arrange contacts between the churches in the belligerent countries. Though their results were but modest, they nonetheless bespeak the growing conviction that the churches should together bear witness in the cause of mutual understanding between the peoples across national frontiers. Above all there were the steps taken after the First World War. That was the period when Nathan Söderblom, Archbishop of Uppsala (1866–1931), who even during the war had been the moving spirit behind many of those proposals, now became the leading figure in the new 'Life and Work' movement. The experiences of the war had disturbed the churches sufficiently to increase their readiness to work together. The problems connected with peace and war dominated the two great conferences mounted by the Life and Work movement in Stockholm in 1925 and Oxford in 1937. Then in 1948 the World Council of Churches came into being through the fusion of the Faith and Order and the Life and Work movements. Ever since then the work of the World Council of Churches has been marked by the commitment of the Life and Work movement.

It was Dietrich Bonhoeffer who most penetratingly formulated the proposal that a council of the churches should bear witness for peace. On 28 August 1934 at a meeting of the Life and Work movement he said during morning prayers: '*How will peace come?* Who is sounding a call to peace that the world hears—is made to hear? That all peoples must rejoice at it? The individual Christian cannot do that. He may indeed raise his voice when all others are silent, and make his witness, but the powers of the world can stride over him without a word. Perhaps, too, individual churches can testify and suffer—if only they would!—but they too would be crushed by the power of hate. Only the one great ecumenical council of the Holy Church of Christ throughout the world can say it in such a way that the world, though it gnash its teeth, has to listen to the word of peace and the peoples rejoice because the church of Christ takes their weapons from their sons in the name of Christ and forbids them to make war, and proclaims the peace of Christ throughout the frenzied world' (Collected Writings 1, p. 219). In making this appeal Bonhoeffer assumed that the separated churches are already the church of Jesus Christ in the togetherness of the ecumenical movement and that they can speak and act as the church of Jesus Christ. But the whole question is whether they and their representatives can seize the opportunity God is offering them.

'We can do it now, today. The ecumenical council has met, and it can issue this radical call for peace to the believers in Christ. The peoples in East and West are waiting to hear it. Must we allow ourselves to be shamed by the heathen in the East? Are we to leave in the lurch the individuals who are venturing their lives on this message? Time presses, the world is stiff with weaponry, and mistrust stares fearsomely from all eyes. The trumpets of war may sound tomorrow—why do we still hesitate? Do we want to be accessories in wrongdoing as never before?'

Bonhoeffer's clarion call had no immediate results, but his idea, though dormant, was not dead. Especially after the Second World War it gained fresh topicality. After the establishment of the World Council of Churches, it was virtually impossible to escape the question of the authority to be attributed to plenary meetings of the Council. Were they a kind of council of the churches? Was not this a forum from which the call for peace of which Bonhoeffer had spoken could go out? The idea received further impetus from the second Vatican Council. A conciliar assembly had taken place, and even though it was limited to the Roman Catholic church, it nevertheless demonstrated that councils can be convened in our times too.

The plenary meeting of the World Council of Churches held in Uppsala in 1968 again expressed the hope that a universal council would be convened. 'The member churches of the World Council of Churches, which are plighted to one another, should work towards the time when a truly universal council can once again speak for all Christians and point the way to the future' (Uppsala report, p. 14). At the same time the plenary meeting spoke of the church 'as the sign of the future unity of mankind'. In other words, a universal council is meaningful only if it contributes towards the unity of mankind. 'Secular society has produced instruments of reconciliation and union which seemingly are often more effective than the church. To outsiders the churches often appear weak and irrelevant, and concerned with their own affairs to the point of satiety. They need a new openness to the world with its struggles, its achievements, its restlessness and its despair.'

In the years which followed, the proposal of the Uppsala plenary meeting was taken further. In particular, one realisation dawned, namely that a universal council of the churches presupposes 'conciliar community'. To be able to celebrate a council, the churches must come closer to one another. A new quality of community is needed. Therefore *the plenary meeting of the World Council of Churches held in Nairobi in 1975* no longer put the main emphasis on a universal council, but on achieving conciliar community among the churches. In so far as the churches allow themselves to be led by the vision of a future council, they will be carried beyond their present divisions and will begin jointly to bear convincing witness.

How realistic is it to speak of a world assembly for justice, peace and the preservation of the creation? Is the time now ripe for a world assembly? Is it possible that the vision which has led the ecumenical movement for decades can now be translated into reality—that, if not an actual council, at least a conciliar assembly could meet, able to speak convincingly about peace? Have Christians grown sufficiently close to one another over the past few years to enable the churches to take this giant step? It seems unlikely that the proposal would be canvassed so widely and so vigorously unless conditions had indeed altered. True, the churches have not come irrevocably closer to one another; indeed, it has become even more evident in recent years that differences of doctrine and church order are unlikely to be overcome in the foreseeable future. Unity will not be proclaimed either today or tomorrow. And yet Christians have become more conscious that they belong to one another. More and more of them are becoming convinced that the churches are being called by their Lord to bear a common witness, and members of all churches can see less and less reason why the existing differences should prevent them from bearing this witness in common. But above all there is a growing consciousness that 'time is running out'. The word of peace must be spoken *now*, and hesitations put aside. *Now* is the time for the venture of faith into joint action.

And yet there is far from being general agreement that the churches are really ready for a conciliar world assembly for justice, peace and the preservation of the creation. The step from the level of the appeal to the level of actual implementation has not yet been fully taken. Many churches have come out with solemn declarations, but few have gone beyond generalisations. Above all, no joint planning has yet taken place. Discussions held under the auspices of the World Council of Churches revolve simply around preliminary questions. No articulation of the common will of the churches has yet been forthcoming. What is the significance of this? Must it lead to the conclusion that, in spite of everything, the time for a world assembly is not yet? That notwithstanding all declarations of sincerity, covert distrust among the churches is still too great? For it could be that in their heart of hearts the churches do not want to meet together in a world assembly: that although they all welcome it in principle, they are happy when another one drags its feet, as this provides welcome confirmation of their own hesitations?

Where are the obstacles, and how can they be overcome? What are the doubts which stand in the way of plans for a world assembly? The objections which have so far been voiced in the discussions may be summarised under three heads.

(a) *What authority can be assigned to a world assembly of the churches?* The fear is repeatedly expressed that a world assembly might arrogate to itself too much authority. Many speakers have urged that a world assembly must not limit the freedom of decision of the individual churches; that such an assembly is not above the churches and cannot take decisions for them. Any attempt to create an ecclesiological *fait accompli* must be forsworn.

The use of the word *council* almost inevitably gave rise to the suspicion that what was being planned was a world assembly which would set itself up above the churches and decide and speak for them. Especially the churches in whose ecclesiological self-understanding the concept of a 'council' has a precise connotation, voiced fears that for the present a common council could not be held. A council presupposes the unity of the churches. A council of churches still separated is a contradiction in terms. The statement of the *plenary meeting of the World Council of Churches in Nairobi in 1975* still had full validity: 'Our present inter-confessional meetings are not councils in the full meaning of the term, because they are not united by a common understanding of the apostolic faith, a common priesthood and a common eucharist' (Nairobi 1975 report, p. 27). They are at most 'pre-conciliar' meetings. They may 'express the sincere desire of the participating churches to be a preliminary sign of full conciliar community and work towards its realisation, and even be a real foretastes of such community' (ibid. p. 28).

For the discussions soon led to the feeling that it would be better to avoid the use of the term 'council', as this could only lead to confusion and cause obstruction. So the word 'council' was replaced by 'convocation' or the even simpler and less pretentious 'world assembly'. Another fear was more characteristic of the evangelicals. Must it not be presumed that the proposed council would in fact be dominated by the Roman Catholic church? Was is realistic to talk about a common, mutual initiative? For the Roman Catholic church so automatically assumes itself to be the one church of Jesus Christ that it has difficulty in participating in joint planning. Would it not inevitably, therefore, look for ways to emphasise its special position? Would it not at the very least seek to appear as the initiator of the action? And would the mass media not assist this presentation? The day of prayer at Assisi for which Pope Paul II issued invitations in the autumn of 1986 shows up the problem quite clearly. It was conceived on the grand scale. It enabled representatives from many churches and religions to spend a day together praying for peace. But the initiative quite clearly came from the Pope. He alone issued the invitations, and the representatives of other religions were his guests. A world assembly convened on this basis would be foredoomed to failure. Many churches would take part in such a meeting either reluctantly or not at all. They would feel themselves to have been taken in.

Given the existence of so many provisos and hesitations, can an assembly that is different from the ordinary meetings of the ecumenical movement that have taken place up to the present be held? Or will the whole proposal eventuate in just another invitation to the churches to attend an international conference, only this time under the banner of *justice, peace and the preservation of the creation*?

Two considerations are important in this connection. The world assembly can be different from earlier conferences if the churches can bring themselves to give it the necessary room for manoeuvre. Certainly it must be clear from the start that the assembly has no jurisdictional rights over the churches. Its authority will consist solely in the weight of the pronouncements it is able to make. Its decisions will have no binding force, and each of the churches will retain the freedom to distance itself from them. Just because they retain this freedom, the churches will be able to allow the world assembly some room for manoeuvre. In view of the dangers that threaten, they can empower it to go beyond the churches and their present witness. They can encourage it not to be content with almost platitudinous statements, but to hold up a mirror to the churches in the light of the gospel. The more freely a world assembly is able to do its work, the more likely is it to say a relevant word that cannot be ignored, based on the gospel.

The second consideration relates to the sponsorship of the assembly. It will be most likely to achieve its purpose if the churches are jointly responsible for it at all stages. The churches must decide to form a joint committee charged with convening, preparing and running the assembly. And since the assembly has no juridical functions, this committee will do its work both in close contact with and also at a certain distance from the individual churches. But the greatest care must be taken to see that the individual traditions receive an equal emphasis. The principle of *par cum pari*, which was established in the decree concerning ecumenism with a view to dialogue between the separated churches, must be followed out strictly in matters affecting the sponsorship of the assembly.

(b) *What theme would be appropriate for the assembly?* The answer to this question was not clear from the outset. The World Alliance of Reformed Churches had spoken of 'justice and peace'. The World Council of Churches had added 'preservation of the creation' as a third dimension. The Conference of the Evangelical Church in Germany wanted a council about peace convened. Many, especially in the West, welcomed this concentration of the matter for discussion. They argued that a world assembly could not deal adequately with more than one subject, and further that the subject of nuclear war was *the* priority—not only for the West, but for the whole world. They held that all the essential points that should be made publicly at the present time could be made in connection with that subject. Others, especially representatives of the third world, take a different view. Important as it is to say a clear word about the nuclear threat, a world assembly—they say—would not be credible unless it gave an equal emphasis to the question of injustice. According to them, the central problem is and remains exploitation, poverty, hunger and oppression. This intervention was successful, and in January 1987 the Central Committee of the World Council of Churches resolved to hold a world assembly on the three themes of justice, peace and the preservation of the creation.

But the clash of priorities will not be resolved simply by bringing them together under a common title. Over the next few years the tension will have to be worked out. Just because of this conflict, the regional conferences will be of the utmost importance. For they provide the opportunity of articulating the priorities as seen in the different regions and thus laying the groundwork for a truly representative world assembly.

(c) *What will the world assembly say?* Will it have anything at all to say that takes matters further? The risk of the undertaking is obvious. How easy it would be for the assembly to become embroiled in disputes, and end in confusion! Or worse still, to emit insignificant platitudes with grandiose gestures! There have already been far too many international conferences that did little more than mirror, with varying degrees of faithfulness, existing interests and the unsolved problems arising from them. What would be the point of adding one more?

The world assembly of the churches is most likely to have something constructive to say if it seeks unflinchingly to bring the spirit of the gospel to bear. It would be an illusion to imagine that the churches possess, as churches, more political understanding than other international bodies. To all appearance they are just as impotent to halt the vicious circle of events as the rest of the humanity which is caught up in it. In the last resort their contribution can only be a recall to the fundamentals on which their life and witness are founded. Of course they must act on the best information available: any pronouncements made by the assembly must be in line with the knowledge of the experts—the *real* ones, not only the self-styled ones. But what must above all distinguish the world assembly from other conferences must be that it approaches the problems in the spirit of the gospel and thereby brings fresh perspectives into the discussion. The assembly can make it clear that faith confers a freedom that can break through both the slanted information coming from interested parties and impotent surrender to the nexus of events. In particular, it can testify to this freedom by frankly admitting the churches' past failures. Its message will be disregarded if it tries to arrogate to itself the right to tell others what they should do. But if the message primarily expresses the churches' own commitment, it will awaken a response. This, however, can only happen if the assembly is backed by the churches and the individual members of the churches. If it is mainly an affair of church leaders and ecclesiastical hierarchs, it will be of no lasting effect. The mass media will give it a brief mention and then go back to the common round. Therefore the grass-roots of the churches must be involved in its preparation. Their questions and anxieties must be taken seriously. The readiness for commitment must find expression at the assembly. The planned world assembly is most likely to be able to fulfil its mission if the mission grows out of this commitment. In so far, and only in so far as the churches, the parishes and the members can see their interest and contribution reflected in the assembly will they be encouraged to go forward along the road of justice, peace and the preservation of the creation.

Translated by Alan Braley

PART I

*Peace in Face of
The Nuclear Holocaust*

Rosemary Radford Ruether

War and Peace in the Christian Tradition

THE PROMISE of peace is central to the biblical and Christian tradition. 'Peace on earth, good will to humankind' is the angels' song at the birth of Jesus. The presence of Christ in our midst is said to bring the 'peace which passes understanding' (Phil. 4:7). Nevertheless, the Christian tradition has held a whole range of views about peace. The split between the spiritual and the historical, which plagues Christian spirituality, is reflected in controversies about whether peace is primarily inward, or whether the quest for peace demands an effort to reconstruct the social order in order to overcome the conditions that create violence between political bodies.

Discussion of peace means also a discussion of its contrary, war. When is participation in war permitted for Christians? In this overview I will assume that peace involves an inter-connection of inward peace and a commitment to ending war and violence in society. Therefore, I will discuss also the views of war, the limits of war and the means of overcoming war in Christian tradition.

The mainline view in Christianity, both for Catholics and Protestants, is that war is justified under certain conditions and with certain limitations of means in order to re-establish conditions of peace. But around this mainstream view there are two other views of war and peace which stand at polar opposites and which have exerted great influence on Christian theory and practice. One of these is pacifism. Although only a small minority of Christian churches take pacifism as normative, this view is often seen as the true Christian ideal. On the opposite pole from pacifism is holy war. Although no church would officially endorse holy war, this view has exerted enormous influence on Christian rhetoric and practice in actual war situations.

All three of these viewpoints have their roots in the Bible. Holy war has deep roots in Hebrew Scripture. The conquest narratives in the book of Joshua depict God mandating holy war against all the people of Canaan simply because they are there, impeding Israelite conquest of the land which God has promised to them. Here 'making peace' means capitulation to Joshua's claim of sovereignty for the Israelites. Those cities who do not capitulate are described as having every man, woman and child, and even animals, put to the sword and their cities burned to the ground.

> For it was the Lord's doing to harden their hearts that they should come against Israel in battle, in order that they should be utterly destroyed, and should receive no mercy but be exterminated, as the Lord commanded Moses (Joshua 11:20).

In the apocalyptic tradition holy war is raised to the cosmic level. The enemies of Israel are presumed to be the enemies of God, representing the Devil, the power of cosmic wickedness. This struggle between good and evil, God and Satan, will culminate in a final apocalyptic battle. The spiritual legions of Satan, and also their earthly representatives in the armies of enemy empires, will be defeated and millennial peace established in a transformed heaven and earth. This apocalyptic language is also found in the New Testament, particularly in *Revelation*. Here the saints sing Hallelujah as the mighty angel of the Lord throws down Babylon, the great city, with violence and obliterates it from the earth. The Messiah appears as a warrior on a white horse, his robe dipped in blood. Surrounded by the warrior angelic hosts, he exterminates the armies of the nations. After a millennial reign, all the forces of cosmic evil are destroyed in a lake of fire and peace is established on a transformed cosmos in which 'every tear has been wiped away'.

This language of holy war has exerted great influence on the rhetoric and imagination of Christian war-making. This language lends itself to fanaticism, since it invites us to view the 'enemy' as enemies of God, and even as devils who have lost all fellow-humanity. It also lends itself to extreme violence by suggesting that total extermination of the others will eliminate evil itself.

Such language is found in the medieval Crusades against the Muslims, in the wars of religion of the sixteenth and seventeenth centuries, and in modern international wars. Colonial conquests of native peoples, such as the Indians in North and South America or the Africans in South Africa have been justified by picturing these 'natives' in the language of the book of Joshua, as the enemies of those to whom God had promised the land.[1]

This language also has greatly influenced the modern state of Israel in its conquest of the land from the Palestinians. Christian support for the state of Israel has often combined a literal acceptance of such Old Testament land claims as a permanent divine gift to the Jews, with apocalyptic imagery of a final cosmic battle between God and Satan that will come about when the return of the Jews to their 'promised land' is completed. Modern Protestant fundamentalists equate this final battle with nuclear war between the 'Christian world' (the United States and a converted Israel) and the Communists. God is pictured as miraculously preserving the elect while destroying the 'wicked' and purging the earth with fire.[2]

At the opposite pole from these views is the Christian pacifist tradition which abjures all participation in war. Yet the peace churches of the left wing of the Reformation, such as Mennonites, Quakers, also share a millennialist tradition. They also look forward to a holy war in which God and his angelic hosts will exterminate the wicked. But they believe that only God can do this. Humans can only sin if they lift up the sword against others, even to defend one's own life.[3]

Peace churches stress non-resistance to evil and an ethic of redemptive suffering. The Christian is called to be a follower of Christ by following the path of non-resistance to evil. Rather than inflicting suffering on those who threaten, the Christian absorbs the suffering of others, maintains an attitude of love and forgiveness toward those who hate and thus participates in Christ's atonement for sin. Hopefully, this stance of love and inward peacefulness will soften the heart of the violent and call forth their conversion from hatred and violence.

This pacifist view finds its chief roots in the New Testament, particularly the Gospels.[4] General condemnations of war are found in many of the pre-Nicene Church Fathers. War is seen as characteristic of the sinful world, while peace is the essence of Christianity. This peace is first of all the peace which has been established between humans and God by Christ. This reconciliation is expressed in relationships of love between Christians. 'Grace to you and peace from God our Father and the Lord Jesus Christ' is the typical salutation of Paul to fellow Christians (1 Cor. 1:3; 2 Cor. 1:2; Gal. 1:3; Eph. 1:2; Phil. 1:2; Col. 1:2; 1 Thess. 1:1; 2 Thess. 1:2; Titus 1:4; Philem. 1:3). Christian peacefulness is seen as anticipating that redemptive reign of God when all dissension has been overcome. Thus Origen says of the Christian lifestyle:

> To those who ask us whence we have come or whom we have for a leader, we say that we have come in accordance with the counsels of Jesus to cut down our warlike and arrogant swords of argument into ploughshares and convert into sickles the spears we formerly used in fighting. For we no longer take sword against a nation nor do we learn any more to make war, having become sons of peace for the sake of Jesus who is our leader ... (Celsius 5.33).

This peacefulness should radiate out to the pagan world as well. The Church Fathers' admonition against violent resistance to those who would do violence to Christians, including the persecutors of the pagan state: the Christian is to return good for evil to those who hate them. For many early Church Fathers, this also meant that Christians should not participate in war. Some Christians did, however, become soldiers in the Roman military by the late second century. Strictures against the legitimacy of Christians as soldiers, found in Tertullian and Origen, mingle general rejections of war with beliefs that participation in the army of a pagan state was illicit for Christians since it involved fighting under the standards of pagan gods.[5]

These criticisms of Christians as soldiers disappeared with the conversion of Constantine and his use of the Christian symbol of the cross as a battle symbol. Indeed, fighting 'under the cross' readily lent itself to the opposite, crusading attitude which saw the wars of a Christian emperor as holy wars, wars of the godly against the wicked. This can be seen in the encomium of Bishop Eusebius of Caesarea on the Emperor Constantine.[6]

It is Augustine who established the view of war in 'Christian times' that was to become normative for Western Christianity. Augustine does not follow the Eusebian tendency to make the Christian state an instrument of the Kingdom of God. Rather, for Augustine the empire, even under Christian emperors, remains distinct from the City of God. Its principle of peace, established through coercion and domination of others, remains alien to that of the reign of God based on love and reconciliation. Nevertheless, within fallen history, the state has a legitimate purpose. Its role is to restrain the violence of evil ones who would assault the civic concord needed by society and rebel against its laws. Christians also need this civic peace. As Augustine puts it, 'as long as the two cities are commingled, we also enjoy the peace of Babylon'.[7]

Not only should the Christian accept this coercive rule of the state for the sake of civic peace by paying taxes and submitting to those in authority, but the Christian should also participate actively in this negative work of 'peace keeping' as governors, generals and soldiers. For Augustine, the Roman Empire was the established instrument of God in maintaining this negative peace of the restraint of evil. All rebellions against its authority were by definition sinful. Thus he even justifies slavery as just punishment for sin, on the assumption that slavery has its origin in the subjugation of those who rebel against the state.[8]

The Medieval Church inherited Augustine's doctrine of the two kingdoms and his justification of the coercive role of the state. Living in an era when the centralised authority of the empire had broken down and all civic order was precarious, the church also attempted to set limits to warfare by promoting the *Peace of God* and the *Truce of God*. The *Peace of God* limited those who could be involved in war. The *Truce of God* limited the times when war could be conducted. For example, the Council of Narbonne (1054) decreed that there could be no attack on clerics, monks, nuns, women, pilgrims, merchants, peasants, visitors to councils, churches, cemeteries and cloisters, shepherds and their flocks, agricultural animals, wagons and orchards. The *Truce of God* decreed that there should be no fighting from Advent through Epiphany, from Septuagesima until the eighth day after Pentecost, nor Sundays, Fridays or Holy Days.[9] Such rules were doubtless honoured mostly in the breach. Also the church had limited power to enforce such decrees. Nevertheless, they set a standard by which the pious knight should live.

Thomas Aquinas formulated the classical Catholic view of the just war, drawing as much on the natural law theory of Aristotle as upon Augustine. For Aquinas, war can only be waged by a duly constituted political authority; private armies are ruled out. The cause must be just, and the intentions of those who wage it must be to punish wrongdoers, vindicate justice, and restore peace.[10] Within these broad guidelines specific yardsticks for the just war were established.

First of all, the cause must be just. One should seek to right wrongs and defend one's community against unjustified attack. Aggressive wars to acquire the territory of others are ruled out. Second, war should be waged only as the last resort. Every effort should be made to adjudicate the dispute by arbitration. Thirdly, there must be feasible ends and means appropriate to the end. Wars that will rage on endlessly, doing far more damage than the original evil they were intended to right, are to be avoided. The goal is to re-establish peace by re-establishing the *status quo* prior to the original violation of justice.

All this sounds much more rational than the actual realities that occasion human wars, where each side defines justice in its own terms, and might, rather than right, has usually prevailed. But these classical principles can suggest guidelines by which an international community of nations might seek to judge just cause and limit the means of war. In the light of contemporary discussion of the legitimacy of nuclear war, it is poignant to recall that the Second Lateran Council of 1139 outlawed crossbows and siege machinery on the grounds of using disproportionately violent means.[11]

Christian pacifism was revived in the later Middle Ages, particularly in revulsion against the violence of the Crusades. The Waldensians, some Franciscans, Wycliffites and one branch of the Hussites rejected war as incompatible with Christian vocation. This medieval sectarian tradition was continued among Reformation pacifist sects: Mennonites, Hutterites, Quakers and Brethren. These Reformation pacifists have continued their witness into the twentieth century. Their members normally refuse to participate in wars of the states in which they reside, doing alternative service or going to prison rather than accepting military service. These historic peace churches have also been the major founders of modern peace organisation, such as the Fellowship of Reconciliation.[12]

However, the just war has not been without its modern advocates as well, even among theologians and Christian ethicists. One of the most notable defenders of the just war tradition against pacifism was Reinhold Niebuhr. Niebuhr had been associated with the Fellowship of Reconciliation, but in the early 1930s he broke with them. He attacked what he saw as the utopian view of society held by pacifists, based on a falsely optimistic view of human nature. Against Enlightenment views of natural human goodness, Niebuhr revived the Augustinian-Calvinist teaching of total depravity of fallen humanity. From this doctrine Niebuhr concluded that altruistic behaviour could only be expected in private interpersonal relationships. Public, social relations are governed by the laws of egoistic self-interest and coercion. The best one can expect in social relations is 'rough justice', not love.[13]

Niebuhr praised the Gandhian non-cooperation movement. But he insisted that it was based, not on classical pacifist non-resistance, but rather was an alternative method of coercion available to dissenting movements. He argued that the success of such movements depended on a certain civilised tradition of government. Since this was present in British rule in India, but absent in Nazism, he argued against Dietrich Bonhoeffer's early hopes of applying such methods to resistance against the Nazis. Thus Niebuhr became a prime architect for a new just war argument for entrance into the Second World War,[14] against Christian pacifists who had believed, after the First World War, that no modern war could be just because of its disproportional violence.

Liberation theology has also reshaped the just war theory to argue for the justice of revolutionary wars. Liberation theologians are by no means uncritical advocates of violent methods of social change. All means of peaceful change through political and economic organisations should be tried. But when a repressive government has blocked all avenues of legal change, and maintains its power through unbridled institutional violence, then they believe that the costs of armed struggle for the sake of creating a more just social system represents the lesser of evils.[15]

In traditional just war theory, just war can only be waged by duly constituted political authorities. Although some possibility of legitimate rebellion against tyrants was accepted in classical just war theory,[16] modern guerrilla armies and counter-armies makes it increasingly difficult to decide when a government's tyrannical behaviour has caused it to lose its legitimacy. How does one decide what revolutionary movement represents the legitimate leadership of a political community in the midst of civil strife? President Reagan's manipulation of the terms 'freedom fighters', for US funded guerrillas fighting against the revolutionary Sandinista government in Nicaragua, while labelling the government itself as 'terrorist', indicates the difficulties of maintaining authentic public discourse about justice in situations of revolutionary conflict.

The advent of nuclear warfare, moreover, has revived the argument, begun after the First World War, that no modern wars can be just because of the disproportional violence of modern weapons. Nuclear weapons alter the context of this discussion, since even the notion of one side 'winning' and another 'losing' become questionable when the means of war threaten the survival of the biosphere of the planet earth itself. Several American churches have written pastoral letters declaring that there can be no possibility of a just war with nuclear weapons.[17]

Nuclear weapons demand a new peace ethic in which the traditional distinctions between pacifism and just war advocacy no longer hold. Principled opposition to all war now becomes the only possible Christian and human ethic. Peacemaking cannot be focused only on questions of disarmament and forging methods of international arbitration. It must seek the causes of war in unjust power relations between rich and poor. It must seek just relations between all humans on the planet and a sustainable ethic of human relationship to the biosphere. Peacemaking in the twentieth century has become the first prerequisite of assuring future life on earth. As the pastoral letter on nuclear crisis and the just peace, issued by the American United Methodist bishops, puts it, peacemaking means the 'defence of Creation'.[18]

NOTES

1. In Cotton Mather's *Soldiers Counselled* (1689), the American Indians are identified with the Amalekites of the Old Testament which the Israelites are commissioned by God to slay. In the Dutch South Africa trek into the backlands, there is a similar identification with the Israelites. See John de Gruchy *The Church Struggle in South Africa*, 2nd ed. (Grand Rapids 1986).

2. Grace Halsell *Prophecy and Politics: Militant Evangelists on the Road To Nuclear War* (Westport 1986).

3. John Howard Yoder *The Politics of Jesus* (Grand Rapids 1972) pp. 78–89.

4. Roland Bainton *Christian Attitudes Toward War and Peace: A Historical Survey and Re-evaluation* (New York 1960) pp. 61–65.

5. Tertullian *de Corona Militis*. See C. John Cadoux *The Christian Attitudes to War* (New York 1982) reprint of 1919 ed.

6. Eusebius of Caesaria *Oration on Constantine* XVI, 8.

7. Augustine *City of God* XIX, 26.

8. Augustine *City of God* XIX, 15.

9. *Op. cit.* Bainton p. 110.

10. Aquinas *S.Th.* II, ii, q. 40 *de bello.*

11. II Lateran Council (1139 AD) canon 29; see also Frederick Russell *The Just War in the Middle Ages* (New York 1975) pp. 70–71.

12. Peter Brock *Pacifism in Europe to 1914* (Princeton 1972).

13. Reinhold Niebuhr *Moral Man and Immoral Society* (New York 1932).

14. Reinhold Niebuhr *Christianity and Power Politics* (New York 1940).

15. Gustavo Gutierrez *A Theology of Liberation* (New York 1973) pp. 108–109; also Robert McAfee Brown *Religion and Violence* (Philadelphia 1973).

16. Thomas Aquinas remained ambiguous about the legitimacy of tyrannicide: *de Regno*; see Bainton, *op. cit.* pp. 108–109; Francis Suarez allowed greater legitimacy for it: *Defence of the Catholic and Apostolic Faith* VI:4. Calvin allowed that a subject did not have to obey a king in anything contrary to God's law: *On God and Political Duty* XXXI–XXXII. The most explicit argument for the Christian right of tyrannicide was formulated during the Puritan rebellion and execution of Charles I: John Milton *The Tenure of Kings and Magistrates* (1649) and *The Defence of the English People* (1651).

17. The National Conference of Catholic Bishops *The Challenge of Peace: God's Promise and Our Response*, 3 May 1983 (Washington 1983); The United Methodist Council of Bishops *In Defense of Creation: The Nuclear Crisis and a Just Peace* (Nashville 1986).

18. *In Defense of Creation* p. 6.

Damaskinos Papandreou

The Peace Documents of the Orthodox Church

THE URGENT problems that occupy mankind as a whole today could not fail to leave their traces on the conciliar movement which in our days is manifesting itself within the Orthodox Church. Already the first preconciliar pan-Orthodox conference which took place in 1976 at Chambésy expressed the wish 'to co-operate with the faithful of other religions in order to counteract every form of fanaticism and to bring to realization the ideals of freedom, of reconciliation among the nations and of peace in the world, in the service of the men and women of today without distinction of race or religion' (cf. *Synodica* III, Chambésy/Geneva, 1979). Beyond this, the same conference put on the agenda of the Great and Holy Council of the Orthodox Church the subject of 'the contribution of the local Orthodox Churches to the realization of the Christian ideals of peace, freedom, fraternity and love between the nations and the elimination of racial discrimination'.

This subject was put on the agenda of the succeeding third phase of the conciliar process by the second pre-conciliar pan-Orthodox conference, which met in 1982, also at Chambésy. In his capacity of secretary for the preparation of the Great and Holy Council of the Orthodox Church the author of this article presented to the inter-Orthodox commission which met at Chambésy in February 1986 in order to prepare the third pre-conciliar pan-Orthodox conference a report which was drawn up taking into account the positions adopted by the various autocephalous Orthodox Churches, and also formulated a synthesis which was intended to represent the pan-Orthodox consensus on this subject. After intensive discussion and revision this report was passed on by the inter-Orthodox commission as a draft text to the third

25

pre-conciliar pan-Orthodox conference which met in November 1986, once again at Chambésy. This conference supplemented the text on a few essential points, especially with regard to atomic war, and passed the document unanimously for submission to the projected Great and Holy Council of the Orthodox Church (cf. *Una Sancta* 42 [1987], pp. 15–24).

The participants at this conference first of all amended the description of the subject as a whole, which now runs: 'The contribution of the Orthodox Church to the realization of peace, justice, freedom, fraternity and love between the nations as well as to the elimination of racial and other forms of discrimination'.

1. THE DIGNITY OF THE HUMAN PERSON: FOUNDATION FOR PEACE

At the centre of this document on peace, which is divided into eight chapters there stands the human person who, in keeping with Christian understanding is focused on God's incarnate Logos (ch. 1). Through the incarnation the Logos has recapitulated in himself the entire creation, that is he has restored once again man's holiness and greatness and has eliminated the causes of all disunity (ch. 3). On this basis man is able to demand a right to dignity. The dignity of the human person is in fact the foundation for peace, justice, freedom, fraternity, and love.

The first thing the document describes is the foundation of peace: 'There is a particular point in beginning by emphasizing that the biblical concept of peace is not identical with a neutral, negative view that would simply identify peace with the absence of war. The concept 'peace' is identical with the restoration of things in their pristine innocence before the fall, when man and woman still lived and breathed in the life-giving breath of their creation in the image and likeness of God. In other words, it means the restoration of relations between God and man, it means peace between God and man.'

For the Orthodox Church the real object of its mission in the world and in the history of salvation was always man; 'crown and summing up of divine creation'. A number of well-chosen references to the writings of the Fathers substantiate this statement of Orthodox principles, which can also count as normative, since it sees itself as a 'call' to 'all men and women of good will' to 'peaceful and creative work' and as a 'duty' to 'co-operate' with all Christians and with the believers of other world religions 'who are looking for true peace' with the aim of achieving 'understanding between different religions' and 'the realization of fraternal relations between the nations' (ch. 1).

2. THE VALUE OF HUMAN FREEDOM

The dignity of the human person and the value of human freedom are mutually dependent. 'The divine gift of freedom is the fulfilment of the human person, and is so to the extent that on the one hand the individual carries within himself or herself the image of the personal God and on the other hand personal community on the basis of the unity of the human race mirrors the life of the holy trinity and the community of the three divine persons.'

A 'superficial view of the human person' can however lead to men and women abusing freedom. 'Through the gift of freedom men and women become conscious of themselves and at the same time become capable of choosing between good and evil (Gen. 2:16–17).' Freedom however is only 'maintained to the extent that men and women decide to be free, but not independent of their creator'. Freedom is a divine gift, but it includes the 'danger of disobedience, of autonomous self-determination in relation to God and thus the danger of falling away from him'.

The abuse of freedom and lack of respect for the human person make room for evil in life and in the world. The text enumerates the manifold expressions and forms of evil in the contemporary world, such as secularization, violence, moral decay, racism, re-armament and wars, the hunger experienced by millions of people, the destruction of the environment, etc. (ch. 2). In view of this threatened situation the world finds itself in, the text expounds the 'duty' of the Orthodox Churches to devote all their efforts to bring out the importance of man as a person, as corresponds to the heart of their understanding of man, so that the 'immense fear in contemporary mankind' disappears in favour of the freedom of men and women (ch. 2 and 3).

3. NO FREEDOM WITHOUT PEACE

The document draws attention to the fact that freedom is unthinkable without peace. 'There is nothing more specifically Christian than to devote oneself to working for peace,' said Basil the Great (cf. *Epistola* 114, PG 32:528). 'Peace' as understood by Christians is that peace 'that one attains in the Church', in other words the peace that Christ promised (cf. John 14:27). It is 'the mature fruit of the summing up of everything in him, of the holiness and the greatness of man made in the image of God'.

In this fourth chapter it is demonstrated with the help of numerous citations from the Fathers that peace and justice go together but that neither can be realized without mutual love. The text comes to the conclusion that only if all men and women work together to bring about the realization of these three factors will 'the hostility and the distrust that poison the international climate' disappear.

4. PEACE AS A MEANS OF AVERTING WAR

In the chapters that follow a declaration is first of all made that Orthodoxy in general condemns war. It regards it 'as a consequence of the evil and the sin in the world. It has only permitted wars as a concession and only if the result was to be the restoration of the freedom and justice that had been crushed. Hence it does not hesitate to declare that it is opposed to any and every form of building up armaments, whether it is in the conventional or in the atomic field or even in space, irrespective of which side is striving for it ... Atomic war [is] inadmissible from any point of view on both ecological and moral grounds. It is a crime against humanity and a mortal sin against God, whose work it destroys.' This is quickly followed by the declaration: 'Nevertheless we are convinced that the investigation and use of space for peaceful and useful purposes are not contrary to the will of God' (ch. 5).

With regard to the elimination of racial and other forms of discrimination (ch. 6) and the realization of fraternity and solidarity among nations (ch. 7) the text refers in particular to Orthodoxy's prophetic mission: the witness of love in *diakonia* or service (ch. 8). 'Every ... attempt to want to see Christ really present among us without looking for him in the person needing our help is empty idealogy' and faith in Christ becomes meaningless.

5. THE MISSION AND TASK OF ORTHODOXY IN THE WORLD OF TODAY

The text encourages the Orthodox Churches 'to contribute through the education of their faithful to the renewal of mankind's spiritual and cultural identity and to the improvement of the general climate and ethos' so that the profound crisis of identity of the contemporary world, which manifests itself in the hunger and poverty that exist alongside abundance and the arms race, can be remedied. To this end the Orthodox Churches want to co-operate with the other Christian Churches and confessions as well as with the international organizations. 'Disarmament would not only remove the danger of atomic annihilation but would also make it possible for sufficient financial means to be available to help those suffering hunger and misery.'

In conclusion the text of this document on peace turns into a kind of proclamation addressed to all Orthodox Christians and Churches: 'Because we Orthodox Christians have access to the significance of salvation we must devote ourselves to working for the alleviation of disease, fear and misfortune; because we have access to the experience of peace the lack of peace in contemporary society must not leave us indifferent; because we have experienced the benefits of God's justice we commit ourselves to greater justice in the world and the overcoming of all oppression; because every day we experience God's grace we commit ourselves to the fight against every kind of fanaticism and intolerance among people and nations; because we tirelessly proclaim God's becoming man and man's being raised to the level of God we commit ourselves to the defence of human rights for all people and nations; because thanks to Christ's act of redemption we experience the freedom bestowed by God we can better proclaim its universal value for all people and nations; because in the holy eucharist we are nourished with the body and blood of the Lord we experience the necessity of sharing God's gifts with our brethren, we understand better what hunger and deprivation mean and fight for them to be overcome; because we await a new heaven and a new earth when absolute justice will reign we commit ourselves here and now to the rebirth and renewal of man and society.'

6. CONCLUDING REMARKS

The document on the Orthodox Church's contribution to the realization of peace should be understood as the first attempt on the part of this Church to work out a theology that clearly and responsibly includes and evaluates the entire complexity of mankind's contemporary situation. Naturally this theology is not something radically new and revolutionary: it is based on scripture and the patristic tradition, which are the foundation of Orthodoxy. But one would do this text an injustice if one considered it solely from this point of view. As the Orthodox theologian Olivier Clément has noted (cf. *Episkepsis* 18 [15.4.1987] 376:8): 'Here ultimately we have to deal with the profoundest and most important text that the [third pre-conciliar pan-Orthodox] conference has drawn up. I emphasize that much courage and great spiritual strength were needed for the bishops of Eastern bloc countries to co-operate in drafting these pages and to sign them. Indeed, the Holy Spirit was really at work here.'

Translated by Robert Nowell

Wolfgang Huber:

Peace Documents from the Protestant Churches

1. BEFORE IT IS TOO LATE

SINCE THE transition from the seventies to the eighties ecumenical Christianity has viewed the threat to peace from the nuclear arms race with new consternation and increased anxiety. The main reasons for this are to be found in the development and deployment of new generations of weapons, in the elaboration of options in waging war and the intensification of political and ideological differences, in the failure of arms control and disarmament negotiations, and lastly in the conflict between the elementary demands of social justice and the costs of the arms race. Nor has there been any decrease in the urgency of protest against the madness of the arms race in the second half of the eighties. It is only with great hesitation that the proposals for arms control and disarmament made by Soviet General Secretary Gorbachev have been taken up in the West. Not least among the reasons for the resistance they met were powerful stereotypes of the enemy. One of the Churches' most important tasks for peace is to try to help overcome these. So, in a new way, the Churches' work for peace is challenged.

The World Council of Churches reacted to the new situation in the transition from the seventies to the eighties by convening a hearing which met in Amsterdam in 1981. The report from this public hearing bears the significant title: 'Before it is too late.' The report records a change in the ethical assessment of nuclear weapons which in the years following has determined theological and ethical discussion in the Protestant Churches. The decisive sentences in this report are:

30

'We believe that the time has come for the Churches to declare clearly and unambiguously that both the manufacture and deployment of atomic weapons as well as their use represents a crime against humanity and that any such action must be condemned from an ethical and theological standpoint. The question of atomic weapons is, because of its consequences and the imminent dangers which it brings with it for mankind, a question of Christian obedience and faithfulness to the Gospel.'

On these grounds the hearing called on the Churches to withdraw support from and approval of policies based on the possession and use of such weapons, and to fight for effective steps towards disarmament.

The full meeting of the World Council of Churches in Vancouver in 1983 repeated in essence the Amsterdam statement which has also featured in many peace documents from Protestant Churches in the last few years. That Christians say 'no' not only to the use of weapons of mass destruction but also to their manufacture and deployment is a statement opening the way to a consensus in the Churches between different attitudes to the ethics of peace. A convocation of the Churches can voice that 'no' with authority.

In comparison with many Church statements of the preceding three decades, the change is considerable. For, since the fifties, the main characteristic of Protestant statements on nuclear weapons was an attempt to distinguish ethically between their use and their threat. Whereas the use of nuclear weapons of mass destruction was considered ethically reprehensible and inadmissible, their threat was considered a morally responsible standpoint for Christians. This ethical recognition of the system of deterrence was, it is true, generally qualified as to its duration. Only for a transitional period should 'participation in the attempt to secure peace in freedom through the existence of atomic weapons' be 'conduct still possible for a Christian' (according to the Heidelberg theses of 1959). But the longer this transitional period lasted, the more this kind of formula made it look as if Christians regarded the system of deterrence as legitimate. With the shift in the late seventies from 'deterrence by retaliation' to 'deterrence by waging war', the Churches were faced with the necessity of reviewing their previous assessment. I will give four examples of this kind of review. The examples come from the Netherlands, the German Federal Republic, the German Democratic Republic and the USA.

2. ETHICS OF BEARING WITNESS

In 1980 the Dutch Reformed Church had already published its recommendation on the subject 'The Church and Nuclear Weapons'. This had emerged from a long process of discussion in the parishes. Its basic thesis was: Christians are required to declare themselves uncompromisingly against atomic weapons. This declaration applies not only to their use but also to their possession. This unconditional opposition must be declared because hope in a gradual reduction in the potential of the nuclear threat has proved to be illusory. The call to use the period of time where deterrence has prevented war in order to achieve political settlements which will facilitate and inaugurate effective disarmament, has remained ineffective. The Church must therefore abandon its position of compromise and, with a total lack of ambiguity, 'oppose those powers and forces which still persist in seeking the answer to world discords in deterrence by mass destruction.' The idea that we are justified in 'protecting our freedoms by basing our security on the violation of creation and on the possible destruction of all that we and our opponents hold dear' is totally rejected. Where creation is being violated Christians are however granted the *status confessionis*: that is a situation in which they are compelled by their witness to declare unambiguous opposition. The consequence of this statement is, in practical political terms, likewise unambiguous: namely that, as the concept of balance has not led to disarmament measures but only to a combination of negotiation and an increase in armaments, so the Dutch Reformed Church no longer sees any hope in this concept. It declares itself instead for the unilateral denuclearisation of the Netherlands—an unambiguous step which should act as a signal for the creation of a new pattern of peace in Europe.

Here, as we find two years later in a corresponding declaration of the West German Federation of Reformed Churches, we meet a form of ethical argument which I would describe as follows: the question of nuclear weapons does not belong in the field of the *ethics of discretionary action*, it is instead the subject of the *ethics of bearing witness*.

3. ETHICS OF INTEGRATION

The memorandum from the German Protestant Church which appeared in 1981 under the title 'The Keeping, Promotion and Renewal of Peace', turned out to be far more restrained than the Dutch document. But it too is unambiguous in many respects. It is unambiguous firstly in its diagnosis of the danger zones which make peace in the eighties a threatened commodity. It is also unambiguous in asserting that political commitment to peace is one of the indisputable duties of Christians, and in concluding that alongside this commitment, when faced by thinking which is predominantly military, peace must be understood as a political responsibility. The memorandum sees ways of safeguarding peace in the strengthening of international cooperation, in moving to a typically non-aggressive defence system and in making efforts towards effective disarmament.

But in the conflict between those who declare themselves ready 'to live without armaments' and those who consider military armaments as indispensable in 'the safeguarding of peace', the memorandum strives for integration. Its aim is to keep open the dialogue between the different options in the ethics of peace. That is why it raises again the formula of complementarity in the Heidelberg theses of 1959. According to this the Church must accept the renouncing of weapons as Christian conduct, but it must also recognise that participating in the attempt to secure peace in freedom through nuclear weapons is also conduct open to Christians. Once more this recognition is conditional on the duration of the situation in which war is prevented by the threat of indiscriminate destruction. This recognition is therefore tied to the condition that it 'is only ethically tenable in a context where all political efforts are directed towards reducing the causes of war, extending possibilities for dealing with conflicts in a non-violent manner, and taking effective steps towards lowering the level of armaments.' But the German Protestant Churches' memorandum does refrain from making use of these ethical criteria in assessing current developments. In particular it refrains from making a clear ethical judgement on the deployment of new nuclear middle-range rockets in Europe. Because to use the criteria it has formulated in this way would destroy the integrative function which is the main characteristic of the memorandum both in its theological basis as well as in its programmatic statements. Its aim is indeed to leave room within the Church for the expression of the range of opinions which characterises the public discussion as a whole.

The memorandum from the German Protestant Church is therefore guided not by the *ethics of a prophetic critique* but by the *ethics of integration*.

4. ETHICS OF CHANGE

The ethics of integration aim at enabling differing individual questions of conscience to be represented in one and the same Church. Questions of this nature—whether a Christian should take up arms or not—have not been the main determining factor in decision making in the German Democratic Republic (GDR); this has been directed rather at the question of what the Church as a community of believers can do for peace. A decisive conclusion was expressed for the first time with total clarity by the Synod of the Federation of Protestant Churches in the autumn of 1982. This said: If the threat to all life 'is silently accepted, then we come into conflict with God the Creator, for He charges us to commit ourselves to the preservation of creation and He excludes the right to its destruction. We therefore have here a case of obedience or disobedience to God.' From this the Protestant Churches in the GDR drew a conclusion which they described as a 'rejection of the spirit, logic and practice of deterrence.'

In the language of belief the word 'rejection' (*abrenuntiatio*) belongs in the movement of change. It is the consequence of *affirmatio*, where mankind professes its faith in God's faithfulness to His creation. It is therefore the reverse of standing up for peace, justice and the future of life. The change towards peace which is revealed in and demanded by belief, includes a process of liberation: liberation from domination by those attitudes and ways of thinking which find their expression in the system of deterrence.

Amongst these there is in particular a concept of security which holds that one's own security can only be guaranteed by the insecurity of one's opponent. In contrast to this the Protestant Churches of the GDR have adopted the concept of 'mutual security'. In this the Christian understanding of the political meaning of loving one's enemy is combined with the knowledge that in the atomic age the increase in risk to one's opponent inevitably becomes an increase in risk to oneself. It is in this sense that the concept of mutual security mediates between theological knowledge and secular understanding. Several statements by the Protestant Churches of the GDR have gone on from this starting point to consider its political consequences. Foremost among these is the creation of an atomic weapon-free zone in Central Europe and the strengthening of political and economic stability in both parts of Europe. A crucial factor in these considerations is the particular responsibility both of German states and of their Churches.

As I understand it, the starting point for these observations is not the *ethics of conformity* but the *ethics of change*. It is however these very ethics of change that can include considerations of political good sense. They translate the *rejection* of the spirit, logic and practice of deterrence into a *gradual renunciation* of the system of deterrence.

5. ETHICS OF RECIPROCITY

In 1986 the Episcopal Church of the United Methodist Church in the USA published a pastoral letter and an explanatory document under the title 'In Defense of Creation. The Nuclear Crisis and a Just Peace'. Both documents carry forward the clarification process, an important milestone of which was the Catholic bishops' pastoral letter of 1983. This example underlines in its own way the fact that decisive new orientations in the theology, ethics and practice of peace are only possible today within the framework of the ecumenical community.

With even greater clarity than was possible for the Catholic bishops, the Methodist bishops refuse to regard a system of deterrence as ethically legitimate. Nor can they approve of an interim system of ethics which still tolerates deterrence for a limited transitional period because that period of time still implies an element of moral acceptance. Instead the bishops propose the ethics of reciprocity. This takes account of the fact that rejecting the system of deterrence in itself alters nothing in the actual existence of that system. The nuclear states must rather remove their nuclear weapons in agreed stages. It is just as impossible to have unilateral security as it is to have a unilateral end to deterrence. The ethics of reciprocity take their guidelines from the concept of mutual security; at the same time they take serious account of the fact that overcoming the system of deterrence is only possible in conjunction with one's opponent. They interpret the actual presence of atomic weapons as an expression of the fact that extensive disarmament has not yet succeeded by means of agreed stages.

The Methodists' documents view the demand for disarmament as belonging to a comprehensive concept of a 'theology for a just peace.' The responsibility for a 'peace with justice' is understood as part of the task of defending creation. The Church is summoned to form an alternative community in an estranged and divided world: a loving internatioal community, capable of peace, the Imitation of Christ.

In such considerations the transition from an interim system of ethics to the ethics of reciprocity takes place. One must of course stress more strongly than the Methodist document does, that, according to Jesus' Sermon on the Mount, it is precisely unilateral benevolent action which reveals the true meaning of the word mutuality. The ethics of reciprocity are not the totality of Christian ethics, amongst whose indispensable themes are the unilateral steps towards loving one's enemy and renouncing force.

In surveying the Protestant peace documents, four examples of which I have outlined above, one can see in their assessment of means of mass destruction a possible consensus emerging, in spite of varying ethical interpretations. In the conciliar process which should lead to the world assembly for justice, peace and the preservation of creation, similar agreements must be worked out with regard to other questions of equally great urgency. Among these are, in particular, the call to overcome war as an institution, the question of the conditions and instruments of world-wide social justice, and finally the task of ending the over-exploitation of nature at the expense of the living potential of generations to come.

Translated by Gordon Wood

Stanley Hauerwas

The Sermon on the Mount, Just War and the Quest for Peace

A
Modest
Proposal
For
Peace:
Let
The
Christians
of the World
Agree That
They Will Not
Kill Each Other

So reads the poster and postcards distributed by the Mennonite Central Committee. Some may feel such a 'Proposal' is in fact far too 'modest'. Faced as we are with nuclear weapons our task is to get all people, Christian and non-Christian, to stop killing one another. Moreover this 'Proposal' seems to overlook the strong relation between peace and justice that so many think necessary if we are to make any progress toward the elimination of war. Instead the 'Proposal' is over-printed on a photograph of one anguished soul comforting another through the familiar act of holding one another—an expression of compassion to be sure, but seemingly a long way from what most mean by 'justice'. Yet I want to defend the 'Proposal' as the most important way we can work for peace as Christians.

The argument I will make is in fact even stranger. For I will maintain not only is the 'Proposal' more in accordance with the demands of the Sermon on the Mount, but the ecclesial presuppositions of the 'Proposal' are crucial for helping us understand and interpret the Sermon. I will argue that the 'ethic' of the Sermon is meant to be taken in a straightforward way, to be interpreted 'literally' once its ecclesial context is properly understood.

It is no secret that much of the theological reflection over the centuries surrounding the Sermon has been a sequence of elaborate and quite sophisticated attempts to show that the Sermon was never meant to be followed 'literally'. For example, the demands of the Sermon, particularly those associated with the antithesis, have been said meant only for a select few. Little exegetical support for such an interpretation has been forthcoming. Moreover, this way of interpreting the Sermon results in a two-tiered ethic that makes the kind of lives most of us live as Christians seem deficient.

A more common interpretation, particularly since the Reformation, is the Sermon's radical ethic as an impossible ideal designed to drive believers first to desperation so that they might realize their only hope is trusting in God's mercy. However, again this interpretation has little exegetical rationale. This manner of construing the Sermon also tends to 'interiorise' the Christian life directly associating our *ethics* with the *motive* of our actions. As a result, a fatal wedge is driven between what we do and why we do what we do, making impossible any coherent account of living virtuously.

To interpret the Sermon as applying primarily to the inner life, or the motives of our action, was the way the Sermon was harmonised with, and even said to demand, the development of just war tradition. Thus Augustine argues in *The City of God* (Book XIX) that civil society simply cannot institutionalise the peace based on forgiveness of enemies. All that can be done in these times between the times is to further the world's *ordo* as the nearest approximation of peace we can have. Just retribution for evil is a 'middle course' having transitional value for educating God's people for a peace that will transcend both retaliation and resistance. Thus Augustine says that nonresistance to evil requires 'not a bodily action but an inward disposition'. (Augustine, *Reply to Faustus* XXII, 767).[1] The problem with this appeal to 'inwardness', however, is how we can at once preserve what Augustine calls the 'kindly feelings' required by the Sermon while acting violently to defend the innocent.

This issue has bedeviled just war theory from the beginning. For if, as Augustine maintains, just war is an attempt to embody the love of the enemy for the protection of the innocent through the agency of the state, then just war in theory is but a theory about exceptions to the general stance of Christians for non-violence. I am not convinced that 'love' can adequately summarise the ethic of the Sermon on theMount, but even if that were the case it is still difficult to see how just war in practice can be consistent with Christian non-violence. Once institutionalised, just war is used to justify the standing armies of states and Christian support of those armies; the way to respond to 'injustice' always seems to require violence. Once this becomes the working presuppositions of most Christians then it is assumed that pacifists, rather than those who would use violence, must bear the burden of proof. Once violence is accepted as a means of love to serve the neighbour, admittedly a strange work of love, it threatens to become a way of life that makes non-violence, either as a virtue or strategy, less likely.

These ways of interpreting the Sermon have been challenged by the rediscovery of the eschatology of the Sermon. This 'discovery' at first seemed to be but another way to undercut any literal reading of the Sermon since it was alleged that the apocalyptic expectations presumed by the Sermon were not fulfilled. This negative result has increasingly been qualified in more recent interpretations. There is no question that the Sermon is eschatologically framed in Matthew (4:23–25), but the assumptions that Matthew (and his community) thereby assumed the Sermon could be followed only at the apocalypse cannot be sustained. Allen Verhey notes Matthew was well aware of the delay of the *parousia* (24:48; 25:5, 19) but that only served to underscore Matthew's concern with the ethos of his community rather than with the final judgment itself. 'The apocalyptic discourse and this vision do not abandon this life, nor do they treat it as a mere parenthesis. It is a time of urgency, certainly, but of *moral* urgency. It is a time of testing, surely, but a time of testing that not only calls for triumph over the temptation of sloth and iniquity but provides an occasion to serve 'the least' and, in serving them, an occasion for serving Christ himself. That is the final test; it is the basis for the final judgment. And already now Matthew is exhorting his community to live in expectation of and in response to that judgment.'[2]

Therefore the recovery of the eschatological focus of the Sermon has increasingly been used by recent interpreters to emphasise the Sermon's moral seriousness. In particular the eschatological focus makes clear that the message of the Sermon cannot be abstracted from the messenger. If Jesus is the eschatological messiah then he has made it possible for us to live in accordance with the Sermon through his death and resurrection. The Sermon is but the form of his life and his life, death, and resurrection is the prism through which the Sermon is to be interpreted. In short, the Sermon does not appear 'impossible' to a people who have been called to a life of discipleship which requires them to contemplate their death in the light of the cross of Christ.

This brings us to the relevance of the Mennonite 'Proposal'. The Mennonite reading of the Sermon, in comparison with those discussed above, is usually characterised as a 'literal' reading. Mennonites are said to believe that the Sermon represents a new law which means exactly what it says. The judgment is usually made that their attempt so to interpret the Sermon in fact shows the Sermon is not a practical ethic for those who wish to deal with the socio-political realities of the world. Thus Robert Guelich suggests some anabaptists 'took a revolutionary tack and attempted to build a new society, the Kingdom of God, based on the Sermon's principles (e.g. Munzer, the Zwickau prophets, the Mechiorists). The majority, however, settled for a radical separation of church and state and a withdrawal from a direct participation in socio-political structures that might compromise the principles of the Sermon (e.g., the Swiss Brethren and the Mennonites). Thus, in their own way, the radical reformers illustrate the impracticability of the Sermon's demands for life in the 'real' world'.[3]

This account is not only historically problematic since the Mennonites certainly did not withdraw of their own accord, but were forced to the sideline. More important, such judgments miss the decisive feature of the radical reformers' interpretation of the Sermon. For it was their contention that the Sermon is not so much a law-like code to be applied casuistically, but rather it is descriptive of the habits and virtues of a community that embodies the peace that Christ has now made possible. The Sermon is interpreted in the light of Matthew 18:15–20, for the peace the Sermon envisages is that made possible by a people who are committed to the process necessary for reconciliation to one another.

It is in this light we can challenge the oft-made contrast between Matthew and Paul. For the unity of the body necessary to celebrate the Eucharist indicated by Paul in 1 Cor. 11 is not different from Matthew's insistence that followers of Jesus must be reconciled if they are to be capable of making an offering (Matthew 5:21–26). The process of reconciliation and forgiveness is the engine that drives the many parts of the Sermon. Only a people who have learned to ask for forgiveness—that is, a people who know the hard task is not to forgive but to be forgiven—are capable of being the kind of community that can support one another in the demanding task of forgiving the enemy.

When the Sermon is divorced from this ecclesial context it cannot help but appear as a 'law' to be applied to and by individuals. But that is contrary to fundamental presuppositions of the Sermon which is that individuals divorced from the community are incapable of living the life the Sermon depicts. To understand the Sermon as an ethic for individuals is to turn the Sermon into a new law with endless legalistic variations. The Sermon is only intelligible against the presumption that a new eschatological community has been brought into existence that makes a new way of life possible.

All the so-called 'hard sayings' of the Sermon are designed to remind us that we cannot live without depending on the support and trust of others. We are told not to lay up treasure for ourselves so we must learn to share. We are told not to be anxious, not to try to ensure our future, thus making it necessary to rely on one another for our food, our clothing, and our housing. We are told not to judge, thereby requiring that we live honestly and truthfully with one another. Such a people have no need to parade their piety as they know in a fundamental sense it is not 'theirs'. Rather the piety of the community capable of hearing and living by the Sermon is that which knows the righteousness that exceeds that of the scribes and Pharisees is possible only when a people have learned that our righteousness is a gift that God gives us through making us learn to serve one another.

Surely this is also the necessary presupposition for understanding the antithesis in Chapter Five of Matthew. To be capable of living chastely, to marry without recourse to divorce, to live without the necessity of oaths, to refrain from returning evil with evil, to learn to love the enemy is surely impossible for isolated individuals. As individuals we can no more act in these ways than we can will not to be anxious. For the very attempt to will not to be anxious only creates anxiety. To be free of anxiety is possible only when we find ourselves part of a community that is constituted by such a compelling adventure we forget our fears in the joy of the new age.

Richard Lischer puts it this way: 'The Sermon portrays a dynamic constellation of relationships—a kind of radicalized *Canterbury Tales*—within the pilgrim community. Because the pilgrims have experienced by faith the assurance of their destination, they are encouraged by its promise and guided by its rubrics.'[4] The attempt to turn the Sermon into an 'ethic' abstracted from the eschatological community cannot help but breed self-righteousness as well as ultimately make the Gospel appear ridiculous. 'Our only hope of living as the community of the Sermon is to acknowledge that we do not retaliate, hate, curse, lust, divorce, swear, brag, preen, worry, or backbite because it is not in the nature of our God or our destination that we should be such people. When we as individuals fail in these instances, we do not snatch up cheap forgiveness, but we do remember that the *ekklesia* is larger than the sum of our individual failures and that it is pointed in a direction that will carry us away from them.'[5]

The Sermon's ecclesial presuppositions are nowhere more clearly confirmed than in the beatitudes. There we see that the gospel just is the proclamation of a new set of relations made possible by a people being drawn into a new movement. The temptation is to read the beatitudes as a list of virtues that good people ought to have or as deeds we ought to do. We thus think we ought to try to be meek, or poor, or hungry, or merciful, or peacemakers, or persecuted. Yet we know it is hard to try to be meek—you either are or you are not. Even more difficult is to have all the characteristics of the beatitudes at once.

Yet that is not what it means to be blessed. Rather the beatitudes assume that there are already people in the community that find themselves in these postures. To be blessed does not mean 'if you are this way you will be rewarded', but that happy are they who find they are so constituted within the community. Moreover, the beatitudes assume we are part of a community with diversity of gifts—a diversity that creates not envy but cooperation and love.

It is only against this background that we can appreciate how inappropriate it is to try to make the Sermon justify an ethic of pacifism or just war as such. The Christians that remembered and lived by the Sermon did not know they were pacifists. Rather they knew as a community they were part of a new way of resolving disputes—through confrontations, forgiveness, and reconciliation. On such a reading, peacemaking is not an abstract ethic but a process of a community made possible by the life, death, and resurrection of Jesus of Nazareth.

There is nothing naive or optimistic, moreover, about such a process. The Sermon does not promise if we just love our enemies they will no longer be our enemy. The Sermon does not promise that if we turn our right cheek we will not be hit. The Sermon does not promise that if we simply act in accordance with its dictates the world will be free of war. 'But the Christian does not renounce war because one can expect intelligent citizens to rally around. They usually won't. The believer takes that stand because the defenceless death of the Messiah has for all time been revealed as the victory of faith that overcomes the world.'[6]

No one has developed this perspective on the ethic of the Sermon more powerfully than Gerhard Lohfink in his *Jesus and Community*. By placing Jesus' mission squarely in relation to Israel, Lohfink rightly reminds us that the reign of God proclaimed and enacted by Jesus is decisively concerned with community. Therefore the radical ethic of turning the other cheek is addressed neither to isolated individuals nor to the wider world. Rather Jesus 'always had in mind *Israel* or the *community of disciples*, which was the prefiguration of the Israel in which the reign of God was to shine. Jesus' requirement of absolute non-violence was thus directly related to society; it had public character. The true people of God, the true family of Jesus, is not allowed to impose anything through force—neither internally nor externally. Members of that people cannot fight for their rights with the means of force which are customary in society and which are often even legitimate. Followers of Jesus should rather suffer injustice than impose their rights through violence.'[7]

Lohfink notes that the locating of the kind of community Jesus addressed in the Sermon is of great importance for contemporary debates about peace. Some argue that renunciation of violence is possible only for individuals who have no responsibility for others; while others argue in principle that all political and social action in the world should follow the rules of the Sermon on the Mount. Yet neither side does justice to the logic of the Sermon as it envisages a third alternative—namely a community capable of ordering its life non-violently in order that the world might know there is an alternative to the violence that is often legitimated in the name of justice.

This third alternative, moreover, cannot be characterised, as Guelich does above, as a withdrawal from secular life and conflict. That might be the case if the Sermon was interpreted as justifying an abstract ethical position called 'pacifism'. But I have tried to show that such a position is simply not 'in' the Sermon. In that sense advocates of just war, such as Paul Ramsey, are right to argue that pacifism and just war are equally valid inferences from the Sermon.[8] But the Sermon does not generate an ethic of non-violence, but rather demands the existence of a community of non-violence so that the world might know that as God's creatures we were meant to live peaceably with one another. Therefore there is literally nothing more important as Christians that we can do for the world than for us to refrain from killing each other.

I am aware that many that hunger and thirst after 'world peace', that are anxious to make nuclear war less likely, may find this interpretation of the peace of the Sermon troubling. I wish I could offer them more but I cannot. As Christians we must confess that we are pacifists not because pacifism promises to create a world free of war, but because we believe God would not have us be otherwise in a world at war. That does not mean that we are not anxious to discover and help create the social and economic structures in the world that make war less likely. Yet our commitment to be a people that provide the world with a 'contrast-society' cannot be qualified when such structures do not exist.[9]

If, however, my interpretation of the peaceable community commanded by the Sermon is right, we at least have a sense of the urgency of the task before us as Christians. For now the ecumenical movement can be seen not just as a theological necessity, but rather as the most significant political act the church can perform for the world. Our disunity and subsequent killing of one another as Christians but condemns the world to even more disastrous conflict and killing. So the unity of the church—and we must remember that our deepest disunity is not between Catholics and Protestants, but that between classes, races, nationalities, hemispheres, etc.—becomes the prerequisite for our serving the world as God's peaceable community. All the more reason for us to pray fervently 'Thy Kingdom come'.

Notes

1. Quoted by L. Cahill in 'Nonresistance, Defense, Violence, and the Kingdom in Christian Tradition', *Interpretations*, 38 (1984) 384.
2. A. Verhey *The Great Reversal: Ethics and the New Testament* (Grand Rapids 1984 91).
3. R. Guelich 'Interpreting the Sermon on the Mount', *Interpretations*, 41 (1987) 119.
4. R. Lischer 'The Sermon on the Mount as Radical Pastoral Care', *Interpretations*, 41 (1987) 161–162.
5. Lischer, 163.
6. J. Yoder *He Came Preaching Peace* (Scottdale, Pennsylvania 1985) pp. 27–28.
7. G. Lohfink *Jesus and Community* (Philadelphia 1984) p. 55.
8. P. Ramsey *Basic Christian Ethics* (New York 1950) 171–184.
9. Lohfink, 157.

Dietmar Mieth

On the State of Peace Discussions in the Catholic Church

1. STARTING POINT: THE NATURAL RIGHT TO THE LIMITATION OF WAR

IN THE moral-theological doctrine of the so-called 'just war' it is not a question of legitimising war but of limiting and controlling it morally. In that respect scholastic doctrine corresponds with ecclesiastical-political attempts in the Middle Ages to limit feuds in favour of general peace. The natural rights doctrine sets standards which are above all intended as *standards of justice*.

The deduction of a just war in terms of natural rights rests basically on two premises: 1. on the right to self-defence and 2. on the protection of the common good as a moral duty of the state which has to guarantee the order of justice and peace. The natural right to self-defence against an unjustified attack is not affected by the ethos of Christian salvation recommending the individual not to claim for himself the right to self-defence. For this does not justify failing to protect the attacked third party for whom one is responsible; still less does it justify the state as the bearer of such a responsibility in leaving unanswered the attack on life, justice, freedom and other institutions of the general good.

Thomas Aquinas sets out *four conditions* for a justifiable war: if the cause is just and serious; if there are no other defence possibilities; if the means are commensurate; and if the defence is appropriate. Such conditions of the justifiable war have in the course of time been interpreted more and more precisely. Today they are topical above all as conditions of legitimate counter-violence. According to the moral philosopher N. Monzel, belligerent defence is only permissible when all means of peaceful, or less violent, settlement are exhausted. Defence may only extend as far as meeting the demands of the attack, 'international customs and agreements made under international law for the restriction and humanising of war' must be kept to, the inevitable evils brought about by war must not be greater than the injustice to be repelled: 'if they are greater and more serious, then the injustice must be borne by renouncing belligerent actions'.[1] J. Messner adds to this that a justifiable likelihood of success must also exist. If even one of these conditions does not apply the doctrine of natural rights determines that the war is no longer just.

Against this two objections are always raised: 1. with such limitations no war at all can be justified, 2. these conditions leave so much room for human interpretation that it would be easy to get round the original intent. That the people's churches in times of national wars each stood on every side behind the belligerents proves only too well the justification of this objection. Nevertheless the doctrine of the 'just war' has persisted up to the present day. It still stands as the basis of the guidelines of the *magisterium* of the Catholic Church after the Second World War.

2. PRONOUNCEMENTS FROM THE ROMAN MAGISTERIUM AFTER THE SECOND WORLD WAR

Now, in so far as it speaks of *peace as non-war*, the doctrine of natural rights in no way shows to advantage the wealth of eschatological peace pronouncements. It restricts itself to containing and preventing war and in this sense it received renewed impetus from the Roman *magisterium* after the Second World War. This impetus is certainly connected with the development of nuclear weapon technology. One can speak here of the application of 'war-ethical principles', intended to promote the securing of peace without at the same time picking out as the central theme all the elements of the demand for peace. Thus, in the first instance, Pius XII amplified the principle of assessing possessions which dominated the traditional doctrine by including the principle of *being able to restrict* military actions.[2]

The question as to the means and the uncontrollable damage of a defensive war comes to the fore. Pius XII: 'If the damage which it (the defensive war) brings in its train is incomparably greater than that of the "injustice suffered" (in a war of aggression), one can be obliged to take upon oneself the injustice (of the war of aggression)' (No. 2366). The Pope regards this condition as being *de facto* fulfilled in the nuclear defensive war (cf. No. 3849. 6366f.). The nuclear defensive war loses the legal title as expressed in the natural rights doctrine which sees the defensive war in terms of justice (see No. 5364. 6407).

John XXIII, in his well-known encyclical *Pacem in terris*, characterised it as 'irrational' still to regard war as the suitable means of restoring violated rights (No. 127). 'Irrational' has in scholastic language the same meaning as 'contrary to moral responsibility'. In a similar sense the pastoral constitution of the *Second Vatican Council* declares: 'The horror and reprehensibleness of war grow immeasurably with the increase in scientific weapons. Actions of war using such weapons can bring about huge and indiscriminate destruction which consequently exceeds all bounds of just defence' (No. 80). It is not just a question of the destructive extent of the means in relation to the ends, but of their indiscriminate nature, something not permitted by the ability of purely military combat to differentiate. Even if the pastoral constitution does not, on the other hand, dispute the right to self-defence (see No. 79), it still determines that this right is dependent on whether the means employed achieve what they are intended to achieve (e.g. living in freedom) and whether these means do not in the last analysis compromise the right itself. The condemnation of total war in the pastoral constitution cannot be clearer. Paul VI resolutely continued this line. As his official statement on the question of disarmament, he had conveyed to the United Nations a papal commission document *Justitia et pax*, in which not only is the arms race branded as 'collective hysteria' but also the Council's doctrine is described as categorical: 'It condemns radically the use of means of mass destruction. This is indeed the only "excommunication" to be found in these texts'.[3]

By no longer granting legal title to the use of scientific weapons the doctrine of the three above-mentioned popes and of the Council cancels the natural rights doctrine of the 'just war' by the assertion and application of this doctrine. It appears as if, with the application of scientific weapons, a borderline has been drawn, in which the interpretation of the criteria of the natural rights doctrine displays a degree of clarity which in fact no longer allows the case to be considered in the light of criteria. Pope John Paul II, in his address to the participants at the International Congress for Moral Theology, follows a similar line with the comment that there are not only absolute moral values but also actions which are always and in any circumstances in themselves forbidden,[4] although in his examples he does not take up the problem of scientific weapons. The application of the natural rights doctrine by the Roman *magisterium* now argues every time with conditions stating 'if that is the case then this must happen'. The popes and the Council were clearly of the opinion that the conditions of complete inadmissibility were given, indeed the guidelines of the Rome *magisterium* really only permit a questioning of the condemnation of such weapon systems at the point where it could be proved that nuclear weapons were commensurate to the situation and can be limited in that situation. It would probably be difficult even today to furnish this proof; yet, in contrast to his predecessors, the present pope, over and above clear calls for peace, refrains from using the limitation clauses of the natural rights 'war-ethic'.[5]

3. DIFFERENT STARTING-POINTS IN THE RECEPTION AND INTERPRETATION OF THE GUIDELINES IN THE CHURCH'S MORAL DOCTRINE

The peace discussion in the Catholic Church in the German Federal Republic reveals how different starting-points can lead to Roman Catholic doctrine being received in completely different ways. The Catholic moral philosopher G. Gundlach, for example, outlined his position in 1959 as follows: 'The disruption in the world's system of laws can ... become of such massive importance ... that it also justifies exceptional, indeed massive action. Yes, even the destruction of an entire people in the demonstration of devotion to God against an unjust attacker can represent such worth that this would be justified'.[6] This opinion has been recently expressed again by *W. Kluxen* and L. Oeing-Hanhoff.[7] Gundlach in his day even thought that he could refer for these opinions to the doctrine of Pius XII: even if 'the only success that remained were a manifestation of God's majesty in his order to which we as human beings owe an obligation, the duty and right to defend the very highest possessions is conceivable. Indeed, if the world were to be thereby destroyed, then that would be no argument against our reasoning. For we have firstly a sure certainty that the world will not last forever, and secondly *we do not have the responsibility for the end of the world*'.[8] obviously Gundlach does not stick to the principle of the appropriateness of the means if it is a question of the right of self-defence in the context of preserving freedom.

The absoluteness of the right of self-defence is in fact just as little maintained by most German moral theologians as it is by the *German bishops* in their Statement for Peace in 1983;[9] but the application of criteria for the conditions of the use of the right to self-defence is, in the sense of a 'crisis ethics' situation subordinated to the possibility that *de facto* the ability to control nuclear weapons and other similar scientific weapons could still be available—so that at least their use as a threat for means of deterrence would 'still' be something that could be legitimised. From this arises a conditional condemnation not only of the use of nuclear weapons, but also of a copy-cat arms built-up or deterrence threat.

The *individual criteria* 'which deterrence must satisfy if it is to be ethical or acceptable' (No. 53) are: 'Already existing or planned military resources may not make wars either more easy to run or seem more likely' (No. 53). 'Only such and so many military resources may be provided as are precisely necessary for the purpose of deterrence directed towards the prevention of war. In particular the military resources may not lead one to suspect a striving for superiority' (No. 54). 'All military resources must be consistent with effective mutual arms limitation, arms reduction and disarmament (No. 54).

A third starting-point leading to a different reception of the moral doctrine states at the outset that *such criteria can no longer be fulfilled*. From this basic assumption it draws political consequences. The differing starting-points can be clearly seen in the attitude to the proposition of the Catholic moral doctrine, namely that *one may not threaten with weapons whose use is not ethically justifiable*, even if in limited conflicts it is conceivable to give ethical approval to the use of counterviolence in an easily comprehensible and distinguishable form. Those who, following Gundlach, support the absoluteness of the right of self-defence will consider even this proposition as a fall from grace and they will prefer to declare themselves for that paradoxical logic according to which one is ethically responsible when one is not ethically responsible, in so far as this prevents a situation arising in which one would have to accept ethical responsibility. Those who argue purely logically, i.e., from the point of view of the consequences of one's actions, will dispute the proof anyway that deterrence as non-war can give any guarantee of the possibility of lasting mutual non-agression. Those on the other hand who formulate the above proposition of Catholic moral teaching with qualifications, but accept it as absolutely binding, must time and again enter into the argument about the criteria for rendering compatible a high level of armaments and the securing of peace. Those finally who fundamentally dispute the possibility of fulfilling such criteria (as has been papal doctrine up to Paul VI) will both *de jure* and *de facto* consider deterrance with scientific weapons as no longer possible. What counts for them is that the defence of higher possessions is no longer possible when the possession fundamental to them all—that of human life as a whole—is put at stake. There are therefore present in German Catholicism completely different starting-points comprising the respective perceptions of knowledge, basic logical arguments, value priorities, subject analyses and finally probably also of a different understanding of the Christian ethos under the word of God. Because of these many-layered perspectives the setting of the argument is often shifted in discussions between the various positions, so that it is difficult to reach agreement.

4. 'JUST WAR' OR JUSTICE THROUGH PEACE?

Moral theologians and moral philosophers in the Catholic Church dispute as to whether the doctrinal concept of the 'just war' is still valid. Remarkably this argument has nothing to do with the different starting-points involved, because supporters as well as opponents of ethical legitimisation of nuclear deterrance refer to that doctrinal concept in justifying their position. Others consider it to be in fact out of date, but in their actual line of argument they arrive at similarly tense conclusions. For the politically relevant ethical options it seems therefore in the last analysis not to be decisive if one sticks close to the natural rights doctrinal concept. R. Schwager speaks of the 'self-cancelling nature of a moral theological model of thought'.[10] That is: 'the natural rights doctrine of the "just war" or of legitimate defence or of justified counter-violence is in fact *not wrong*, but in view of modern warfare it has become meaningless',[11] because the doctrinal concept of the 'just war' presupposes: 1. for the responsibility of each individual a time to reflect and the observation of formalities at the start of a war, things which today have shrunk to minutes and seconds; 2. an international authority to see that the criteria are kept to; 3. that something can be assessed that *cannot be assessed today*; 4. the doctrine was intended for the dispensing of justice and peace negotiations *after the event*, no longer likely in a post-conventional war; finally the basis of the doctrine of the just war, namely the natural rights doctrine of *the inalienable right to self-defence, has become meaningless* because modern totalitarian war puts at risk what one professes to defend: one's own life and fate.

Against this line of argument the moral philosopher F. Klüber points out— not unjustly—that it is wrong to maintain that the Council has, under the impact of nuclear warfare, given up the doctrine of the 'just war' as being now meaningless and unusable. Rather he maintains that, 'The *magisterium*'s condemnation of nuclear defence is unassailably covered on all sides, because it holds fast *strictissime* to the central norms of the doctrine'.[12] But there is also without doubt good reason for there having been no further recourse to this doctrine since the Second Vatican Council at the latest. The doctrine has fulfilled its meaning and in so doing has at the same time lost it. True its validity remains as a natural rights doctrine (and therefore its continuing relation to the commitment contained in the Sermon on the Mount will also have to be discussed), but this validity moves from the area of national war ethics to the realm of counter-violence within the state and its legitimisation. The signs are increasing that a 'self-cancelling' (in a positive sense!) of the doctrine of the 'just war' represents at the same time a 'Kairos' for it: in the sense of a renewed confirmation of belief for Christian ethics, the doctrine of peace in the Sermon on the Mount can, as it were in the penultimate moment, be perceived in its eschatological 'now'.

The peace discussion of recent years lays particular value on the *relationship between justice and peace*. If one goes beyond the context of the pure justice of defence, a context which controls the criteriology of the doctrine of the 'just war', one comes up against justice as *a demand for peace* and as *the securing of peace*, and—not least—as also *a sign of hope for peace*. In this sense the statement by the German bishops '*Justice creates peace*' (1983) had introduced the biblical understanding of peace as the 'work of justice' (Isa. 32:17) into its fundamental thinking (No. 11f.). In the discussion among Catholic peace groups like Pax Christi this connection is also stressed, but over and above that it is also understood that peace must also be seen as a conditional preparation for a more just sharing-out in the world. Spiralling armaments hinder a just order in the world economy.

A second emphasis in Catholic peace discussion arises out of a reconsideration of the relationship between so-called 'natural' morality, which produced the natural rights doctrinal concepts, and the historical *belief-ethos* or Christian orthopraxis. In the circumstances of the biblical inspiration of Christian peace groups, the reconsideration of the Sermon on the Mount, and the adoption by liberation theology of socio-ethically motivated pronouncements of belief, we find that the historical contrasting experience with a threat of universal destruction and the concomitant ambiguity of methods of securing peace becomes the starting-point for a realisation in concrete terms of *the commitment indicated in the Gospel*. In this sense the delegates at the German meeting of Pax Christi in 1985 declared 'that conscientious objection becomes an ever clearer sign of practical action for peace'.

In Catholic exegesis the question of *unilateral renunciation of violence* is being freshly discussed not only in terms of an individually ethical sign but also as a socio-ethical concept. Some interpret the ethos of Jesus as a local ethos (G. Lohfink), others as a world ethos (P. Hoffmann). In concrete terms it is a question of the relevance of Jesus's call to love one's enemies and renounce violence in the present political situation in which churches as well as individual Christians take a responsible part in political decision-making processes.

A third problem which arises in connection with the actual peace discussion is the *practical confirmation of belief* for Christians who must discover in their different starting points that they differ not only in the area of factual assessment—of basic ethical systems—but also on the level of practical understanding of belief, even right across denominations. The historical discussion of human freedom and dignity did not always find Christians on the side of the gospel. The question of a 'Peace Council', in itself already raised by the Catholic Diocesan General Synod in the German Federal Republic and again raised under that title by the Protestant Church Congress in 1985, remains a pressing one despite all the hindrances in matters of definition, strategy and organisation.

Not least the peace discussion has led to a renewed discussion today in the Catholic Church as well of the question of 'non-violent resistance' or 'civil-disobedience'. As the theses of the Bensberg district put it: 'Bensberg District shows solidarity with democratic resistance, going as far as civil disobedience if this seems necessary as a last means towards the cause of maintaining and promoting peace and if non-violence is strictly maintained'.[14]

5. ETHICAL OR PRACTICAL COMPROMISE

Our incomplete survey of the state of Catholic peace discussion would lack an essential element if it were to ignore the question of *the relationship between conviction and compromise*. The formulation of this question was the theme of the German speaking international congress of moral theologians in Trier in 1983.[15] In the discussion of peace there is constant reference to crisis ethics, provisional ethics or compromise ethics. Of course nuclear weapons cannot in fact be eliminated overnight by condemnation from the *magisterium*. The question is, what does one do if the factuality cannot be eliminated by simply passing judgment on it? It seems to me that what is needed here is neither a special doctrine of ethical compromise nor a provisional ethic. Ethical judgments are right or wrong; if they are right, then they are valid. In this connection there must be no dilemma between Christian conviction and Christian responsibility. If it is a question of carrying through politically the practical realisation of what is morally right, then it is possible out of ethical conviction to make practical compromises which are not at the same time ethical compromises. Ethical criticism of existing practical compromises in politics and society then remains a constant challenge to change existing practical compromises. All the same the question remains whether the practical application of the criteria I have mentioned would not have to lead to further lack of compromise in the practical realisation of ethical principles as well.

Translated by Gordon Wood

Notes

1. N. Monzel *Atomare Kampfmittel und christliche Ethik* (Munich 1960) p. 52.
2. Documents quoted according to A. F. Utz/J. F. Groner (Ed.) *Aufbau und*

Entfaltung des gesellschaftlichen Le-bens. Soziale Summe Pius XII. 1–3 (Freiburg 1954–61).

3. *Osservatore Romano* 3.6.1976 quoted according to F. Klüber (note 5).

4. See *Osservatore Romano* German edition 9.5.1986.

5. See F. Klüber 'Friedenspolitik im Zwielicht. Spricht Rom deutlich genug?' in: *Katholische Kirche—wohin?* ed. v. N. Greinacher/H. Küng (München/Zürich 1986) pp. 59–77.

6. In: *Kann der atomare Verteidigungskrieg ein gerechter Krieg sein?*, Studien und Berichte der Katholischen Akademie in Bayern 10 (München, 1960) p. 120.

7. See W. Kluxen, 'Gewalt und Gewaltanwendung' in: *Die politische Meinung* 28, 1983, No. 209 pp. 39–50; L. Oeing-Hanhoff 'Ist die atomare Abschreckung unsittlich?' in: *ThQ* 165, (1985) pp. 53–55.

8. See G. Gundlach *Die Lehre Pius'XII. vom modernen Krieg* in: StZ 164 (1958/59) pp. 1–14.

9. In: *Bishops on Peace*, Pastoral Report from the Episcopal Conferences in the USA, Holland, the GDR, Austria, Hungary, Switzerland, Ireland, Belgium and Japan (1983) pub. by the Secretariat of the German Episcopal Conference Stimmen der Welt Kirche No. 19.

10. See R. Schwager, in: *Atomrüstung—christlich zu verantworten?* ed. A. Battke (Düsseldorf 1982) pp. 51ff.

11. See D. Mieth, in: *Atomrüstung—christlich zu verantworten?* loc. cit. pp. 42.

12. See F. Klüber, op. cit., p. 63.

13. P. Hoffmann *Tradition und Situation.* On the 'binding nature' of the commandment to love ones enemies, in the Synoptic tradition and in the contemporary peace discussion ed. v. K. Kertelge (Freiburg/Basel/Wien 1984) p. 111; see G. Lohfink, *Der ekklesiale Sitz im Leben der Aufforderung Jesu zum Gewaltverzicht* (Mt. 8, 39b–42; Lk. 6,29f.), in ThQ 162 (1982) pp. 235–236.

14. See Bensberger Kreis (ed.), *Frieden—für Katholiken eine Provokation?* (Reinbek 1982).

15. See D. Mieth, 'Chistliche Überzeugung und gesellschaftlicher Kompromiß' in: H. Weber (ed.), *Der ethische Kompromiß* (Freiburg 1984) pp. 113–146; see also by the same author 'Friedenssicherung durch Abschreckung?' in: *ThQ* 165 pp. 318–322.

PART II

Justice in Face of Mass Poverty in the Third World

Jon Sobrino

Unjust and Violent Poverty in Latin America

POVERTY IN Latin America is massive, scandalous, unjust and increasing. It is in itself violence against the poor majorities and inevitably leads to violent conflicts. It is in itself a crime against peace. This well known and often repeated fact is the subject of this article, whose purpose is to stimulate a true ecumenism fighting to wipe out unjust poverty and thus effectively promote peace.

1. POVERTY AS DENIAL OF LIFE

For the last twenty years it has been clearly stated that what is most flagrantly wrong in Latin America is 'the wretched poverty marginalising large human groups' (Medellin, *Justicia* 1), that 'the most devastating and humiliating scourge is the situation of inhuman poverty in which millions of Latin Americans live' (Puebla 29). Quantitatively speaking, there is no doubt that the Latin American continent lives in great poverty and faces a future in which poverty will grow even worse. Although we can speak of certain advances in formal democratisation in some countries, this has not produced real democracy—the right to life for the majorities. On the contrary, the economic order in Latin America and the world, the huge and growing foreign debt, resources dedicated to weapons and destruction, including economic destruction, producing wars (El Salvador, Nicaragua) make poverty even worse in these countries as a whole, and create an ever greater number of poor people. By the end of the century, one third of the population, some 170 million Latin Americans, will be living in extreme poverty, biological poverty. It will be very difficult to meet subsistence needs, not to mention other primary needs such as a livelihood, health and education, which are even more difficult to supply. This poverty is quantitatively enormous and qualitatively horrific. We need to remind ourselves of the kind of poverty we are talking about, because poverty does not signify to the same degree in different parts of the world. In the first world there is poverty which may grow worse according to circumstances. But in this case the term is related to something positive, a state of well-being which is attainable and possible if society is properly restructured. In Latin America poverty is related to the negative and *to absolute negation*. It is not a situational lack or falling short of a certain state of well-being but means coming close to death, which has nothing rhetorical about it. The present unjust structures produce slow but real death for the poor majorities. And when they try to resist, then death comes in the form of repression, swift and violent death. The *analogatum princeps* of poverty is *poverty which comes really close to death*. This is the kind of poverty we have in Latin America and in other parts of the Third World it can be even worse.

This poverty is becoming increasingly difficult to conceal. Statistics available to all proclaim it, periodically the media castigate it to stir public opinion and—most recently of all—the poor themselves have begun to make their voice of protest heard. Twenty years ago Medellin said that 'a muffled cry is surging up from millions of people' and this cry is now 'clear, growing louder, more insistent, and sometimes threatening' (n. 89). Since then the cry has become louder still. No tinkering political reforms have been able to suppress it. The silent and powerless resignation of many of the poor is no proof to the contrary. Poverty is real and cannot be hidden. Paraphrasing Paul we can say, 'There is no excuse'; because the world knows poverty.

2. POVERTY AS DENIAL OF PEACE

Poverty is not just a denial of life; it is a denial of peace. Even if poverty's fundamental cause was a scarcity of natural resources, this might still generate some kind of violent struggle to survive, such as occurs in the animal kingdom. But because poverty's causes are historical, it almost inevitably breeds violence, and thus becomes the denial of peace.

First and foremost poverty denies peace because it is in itself violence done to the poor, violence against their lives and most fundamental rights. Unjust structures are the primary and most fundamental form of violence, 'institutionalised violence' (Medellin, *Peace* 16) and the most important cause, at least in Latin America, of all other forms of violence. If peace is the fruit of justice, it is not surprising that violence is the fruit of injustice. The present world order is very unjust and therefore of its nature very violent.

When to objective conditions of unjust poverty are added subjective conditions (awareness, understanding of poverty's causes, the overcoming of resignation, belief that poverty can be eradicated) then, justly, the poor take a stand against it, which, though not always necessarily, gives rise to other forms of violence. Historically this has been the violence of 'national security', in its grossest forms which have prevailed in Latin America over the last few years, or in its subtler forms which also still operate. Then we get state terrorism by means of armies and paramilitary forces. Against the violence of injustice and the added violence of repression liberation and revolutionary movements arise. These may resort to armed struggle, to which the government forces reply in kind. This releases a spiral of violence taking the form of civil wars with ever growing international involvement. We should not forget that since the Second World War there have been no less than one hundred wars in the Third World. Some consider these wars have killed almost as many as died in the world war.

Wars and armed struggles are the most obvious forms of violence in Latin America but the most flagrant violence, which explains almost all the rest, is unjust poverty. The structures generating it become genuine idols, which need sacrificial victims in order to survive; so they produce them. Thus, once conflicts arise, society is not fundamentally divided between violent and non-violent but between perpetrators and victims of violence, oppressors and oppressed. This is a denial not only of the Christian ideal of creation and life but also that of the kingdom of God, human fellowship.

3. ECUMENISM FOR THE SAKE OF JUSTICE

The above is clear and generally accepted in theory. We are thus obliged to respond; and indifference becomes scandalous. Without justice to wipe out poverty and make life viable for the majority in Latin America, there can be no peace. The *option for peace*—to which all pay lip service—has to be an *option for justice*; which fills many with dismay, either because it threatens their illegitimate interests or because of the difficulty of the task. Perhaps the current violent conflicts in Latin America have the tragic advantage of making quite clear how intolerable the present situation is and that its roots lie in the dire poverty we have described. But the obstacles are alarming. There is a very common tendency to interpret Latin American conflicts as ideological, according to an east-west ideological schema and take sides accordingly. This conceals the reality of the situation, makes it more difficult to solve conflicts, and causes poverty to increase. Above all what is required is an *option for the poor against their poverty.*

If this option is not taken, then what is at stake for the world as a whole is this:

On the ethical level: humanity would be objectively and structurally in a state of sin, which can be considered mortal because it brings real death to millions of human beings. Humanity should ask for forgiveness and make amends for the poverty it has caused in the world. And if it lacks the courage to do this at least it must not remain indifferent to the spread of poverty.

On the religious level: the central minimum core of many religions is being ignored. Certainly this is true of the Abrahamic religions: without life God's creation has no meaning; without a just life, human fellowship and the kingdom of God is not possible. It would be completely inconsistent to profess a religious faith and not make a decided option for the life of the poor.

On the human level: the lives of hundreds of millions of people are at stake. Also at stake in this catastrophe is the human feeling of us all. If we do not act in support of life for the poor, if as individuals or nations we concentrate just on our own problems, whether we are aware of it or not, we risk becoming impervious to human feeling. As Paul tells us, if we imprison the truth of reality by injustice, our hearts are darkened, we do not see things clearly, and human beings become inhuman. Of course love would be the best reason for seeking justice and opting for the poor of this world. But at the very least we should do so from self interest, because if we don't we will become inhuman ourselves.

The purpose of these reflections is to encourage a Latin American initiative to call an ecumenical council for peace. Both the World Council of Churches and Pope John Paul II at Assisi have expressed the universal desire for peace and the universal need to work for it. What we want is that this universal desire should seriously take into account the universal struggle against injustice.

Whatever form this meeting may take, it is important that it should be ecumenical so that it can take up the ecumenical cry of the poor. It is also important that it should respond to this cry from the depths of the Christian faith. The cry of the poor is the present historical voicing of Jesus' own cry: 'My God, my God, why have you forsaken me?' The basis of every council has been a question of history and theology. And it will be of this one too. The radical question for faith today is not 'How can we encounter a loving God?' or 'How can we be believers in a secularised world?' but 'How can we be Christians and human beings in a world where there is so much misery—and what must we do about those who are being crucified?'

To answer this question there are certain minimum requirements. First the proclamation of faith in God and what God we believe in. If former ways of seeking and speaking about God were guided by the former questions, namely, 'How can we encounter a loving God?' and 'How can we believe in a secularised world?', now the most basic reality—the scandalous poverty existing in the world—demands a reformulation of our faith in God. As a bare minimum we must proclaim him as God of a just life, and God of peace; we must give priority to active and effective mercy towards those who are crucified by poverty; we must practice that justice which is knowledge of God. This is not the whole of faith, but without it it would be difficult to proclaim God today; and saying we believed in God would have little meaning.

The second requirement is an ecclesial option for the poor. The church must concentrate and fulfil its mission and identity on this basis. This now is the way to make Vatican II's statement on the church come true: that the church is the sacrament of salvation and unity of the whole human species. Again this is not all the Church is and must do. But without it the church becomes disembodied from the real world, it takes refuge in a cosy ecclesiological docetism, abandoning the world to its sufferings, or even acting against the world and adding to them. If it makes an option for the poor the church recovers an identity, a credibility and a relevance.

The third requirement is an ecumenism which is as universal as possible, and certainly Christian, based on these points. It is an ecumenism from the other way round. It starts with the historical reality and goes towards the ecclesial, from what is down and out in history up to the heights of faith. An ecumenism based on the universal cry of the poor, and prepared to answer it, has historical credibility and the potential to bring the churches closer to what is fundamental in the faith. And perhaps this will be a more useful way to unite the churches in other secondary matters which divide them today.

This ecumenism is an ethical requirement which is bound to be beneficial to the poor of this world. But it can also be beneficial to the churches' own Christianity. It is a scandalous truth of faith that in the poor there is light and the poor preach the gospel. From them we receive humanity, hope, courage, love of life, human feeling; and as Christians—as many in Latin America attest—we also receive faith and forgiveness, the witness of martyrs. Either way, from the poor we receive the demand for conversion. Without it neither individual believers, nor the churches nor the ecumenical movement can subsist.

CONCLUSION

All this is well known. We need a detailed analysis of poverty, the remedies for it, and of what the churches must do. We have merely attempted to sum up once more the tragic reality of injustice which creates poverty and which, certainly in Latin America, is the main enemy of peace.

There are no easy solutions or recipes. But to encourage us to seek them and put them into practice let us recall two pithy sayings of Monsignor Romero: 'We must defend the minimum which is God's maximum gift: life.' 'Let us not forget that we are human beings and that here people are dying.'

Translated by Dinah Livingstone

Hans Diefenbacher

Armaments and Poverty in the Industrial Nations

1. WHAT DO WE SPEND ON ARMAMENTS?[1]

SEVERAL DIFFICULTIES stand in the way of any attempt to find out what industrial societies pay for armaments. Even the orders of magnitude involved are such that any numerical assessment is obsolete almost as soon as it is proffered. The 1985 figure for international expenditure for military purposes of some 663,000 million US$ cannot be faulted as an overestimate. About five-sixths of that sum are to be attributed to the industrial nations, and approximately one half of this expenditure is to be ascribed to the super-powers alone.[2] Whatever arithmetical device is used to make these magnitudes conceivable, we feel that such figures are just beyond our grasp. 663,000 million US$—that is far more than the national revenue of the approximately two thousand million inhabitants of the People's Republic of China, of India, and of Indonesia; that is, more than the monetary value of what all those people have produced over the same period. 663,000 million US$ means almost two million dollars a day, and that means that in all but four days the expenditure on armaments amounts to the gross national product of the approximately 20 million inhabitants of the Sudan. Similar attempts to suggest equivalents can be multiplied almost at will, above all in regard to expenditure. How much does it cost to build and equip a school? Or a small hospital? If there were no such military expenditure, what would the money be used to finance?

Because military expenditure is so vast, the second problem has almost to be relegated to the background. Checking and analysis of expenditure on armaments in individual countries confronts one with a series of problems when demarcating figures.[3] What in individual countries counts inclusively as expenditure on armaments and what does not? What statistical arrangement of the figures is to be adduced as a basis for comparing one nation with another in this regard? To offer merely one example: expenditure on armaments in France, expressed in French francs, rose by 11.49 per cent between 1982 and 1983. But if the total is given in US$, then a 3.86 per cent drop in expenditure may be calculated.[4] As long ago as 1972, the Stockholm International Peace Research Institute stated in a publication that the first attempt had been made to assess on a world wide basis the resources used for military research and development.[5] The available data and statistics have become much more comprehensive in the last few years. But since the relative rating of various states has become much clearer, at the same time there has been a growth in the temptation to interpret reality, by one means or another, by presenting data in a specific way.

Hence the Federal budget in West Germany features plan No. 14, which specifies the defence budget. There are, however, many other individual projects in the budget, and other items of expenditure which serve the ends of defence.[6] To cite examples, there is expenditure on the armed forces in project 02 (German Federal Parliament = Bundestag), a NATO member's contribution in project No. 03 (Federal Council of Ministers = Bundesrat), and the cost of Federal border defence in project 06 (Ministry of the Interior). Arms-related ventures proliferate, especially in the budget of the Federal Research Ministry. In other instances it is more difficult to make valid calculations. Hence the evolution of the Federal budget in recent years has been considerably affected by the rapid increase in the cost of the national debt; that is, by interest due and redemption payments. Project No. 32 (Federal national debt) is by now the third largest in the entire budget. Since in past years the national budget as well as some parts of defence expenditure were financed by these debts, essentially, in accordance with the principle of causation, debt service payments must also be ascribed in part to the defence budget. But that kind of attribution does not occur in the national budget.

Of course, a precise account of the amount and the proportion of the national expenditure devoted to the military budget is required to assess the overall economic consequences of this sector. Nevertheless, it suffices to state the order of magnitude and development of this expenditure in relation to other macroeconomic indicators, in order to, describe in principle how the arms budget works. These data are available:

—Arms expenditure has reached an historic high level.

—In the last ten years, the growth rates for arms expenditure were often above the growth rates of the entire budget. It is the super-powers precisely that establish high growth rates.

—Finally, in so far as projected commitments to arms expenditure are available, they generally provide for more increases. At any rate, in no instance is there any mention of a drastic reduction in allocations under this budgetary head. Financial projections still reveal no trace of the will to disarm.

2. ARMAMENTS AS A PUBLIC BENEFACTION

I have used the terms military expenditure and defence expenditure as synonyms, for I wished to emphasise the point that no one uses these funds for any purpose other than defence against attacks by various other states on one's own country. I thereby exclude the possibility that arms expenditure is initiated in order to injure other states: even, indeed, in order to appropriate economic resources of those countries for one's own ends.[7] In the perspective of an essentially neo-classicist economic theory, state expenditure for defence purposes on this assumption is made with only one aim: a country's citizens believe that their well-being is advanced when they are convinced that they are protected from the attacks of other states. This welfare function of defence expenditure has a beneficial aspect which I would term 'public security', the presence of which affords citizens—or most of them at least, and to a determined extent at least—a certain positive advantage. 'Public security', to be sure, is a typical public benefit which, in Samuelson's definition[8] 'all enjoy in common in the sense that each individual's consumption of such a good [in a specific state] leads to no subtraction from any other individual's consumption of that good [in the same state] ...'. Accordingly, the provision of a requisite degree of 'public security' in the sense of the theory of collective goods is a task to be entrusted to the state.

This theoretical classification is no mere exercise in mental gymnastics. It helps us basically to specify three very simple contexts:

The citizens of a state require 'public security'—but not tanks, rockets or guns; guns are only a limited part of the means which have to be applied as efficiently as possible in order to attain the desired degree of 'public security'. But as I have said, there are other means. For instance, a successful disarmament process could reduce instances of arms potential, and thus expenditure, without that leading to a corresponding loss of 'public security'.[9]

Citizens do not demand every possible degree of 'public security'. Just as there is no readiness to finance however many fire services to prevent all possible disasters by fire, in the case of 'public security' the law of diminishing marginal utility applies. Every additional 'unit of public security' involves an accrued advantage which, however, grows constantly smaller the more of this advantage is already present. After a certain point it is even possible to conceive of a negative marginal benefit. But it does not seem always to be guaranteed that expenditure and yield for the armaments budget are measured by this yardstick.

Public security is not the only public benefit which features as a civic utility: the provision of educational institutions, a properly functioning health system, and a satisfactory social security system, are some of the many other public utilities. If limited means are assumed, then an optimisation of the welfare function means competition among these applications for the available funds. These funds are also restricted because, of course, there is competition between the use of means for private and for public benefits. Every penny which is used by way of taxation and contributions to finance public utilities is no longer available for private consumption or investment. ... In economic terminology: in the case of each decision about the extent and type of state expenditure (for arms, say) their opportunity costs would have to be taken into consideration—and this leads to the question whether an alternative use of these means would not lead to a much greater increase in civic welfare than the 'access' of 'public security' which can be achieved thus.[10]

My thesis is now that—first—these three simple contexts are inadequately represented in the decision processes for military expenditure. In addition however—second—the specific effects of a high military budget on the national economy (in other words, its opportunity costs) are usually inappropriately assessed. If my second thesis is correct, in accordance with which the estimation of opportunity costs of high arms expenditure would turn out to be too low, then the decisions are based on false premises. In subsequent sections, therefore, I shall try to describe some major general economic mechanisms of the effect of high arms expenditure.

3. ARMAMENTS, TECHNOLOGICAL PROGRESS AND LIVING STANDARDS

In the last section I stressed the fact that all state expenditure for defence purposes necessarily competes with other state expenditure. This expenditure thus considerably restricts a country's room for manoeuvre.

This competition is especially problematical in this area, since here the yield of arms expenditure in respect of its possible value for the satisfaction of the material needs of the population, and for further economic development, differs essentially from the return on other national or private expenditure.[11] Since arms expenditure does not increase the total of individual or collective consumer goods, it does not improve existing human living standards as does expenditure on nursery schools, theatres, hospitals and so on. Every citizen profits—even if he or she is healthy—from the 'public benefit' of the health service. He or she is assured of care should the need arise. If such a necessity arises the hospital represents a 'direct advantage' for the individual. For him or her it becomes almost a private benefit. ... There is nothing equivalent in the case of expenditure on armaments. Beyond the provision of 'public security' there is no use for arms and associated products; hence there is no direct positive external effect of such expenditure.

In addition, arms expenditure is 'non-reproductive'.[12] It restricts the material development potential of a society. To be sure, the armaments industry is often described as the engine of technological progress, bringing as it does a number of 'spill-over' effects for the civil sector.[13] But several investigations show, on the basis of numerous arguments, that comparable research and development expenditure in the civic area would probably have brought greater advantages. Civically advantageous 'spill-overs' are generally 'expensive by-products which were developed "off the main tracks"',[14] and which are oriented to a technological standard usually unattached to any means of production or consumer benefit.[15]

The effect of non-reproductive expenditure is cumulative with time. If the present economic resources of a country are devoted to military expenditure, then the possibility of providing economic resources in future years will be limited—quite irrespective, of course, of the application of those resources. The cumulative effect occurs if some part of this reduced base is once again applied to non-reproductive expenditure.

4. ARMS AND UNEMPLOYMENT

There is no doubt that, because of its non-reproductive character, arms expenditure can considerably weaken material development potential in the long term. Nevertheless, as part of state expenditure it can revivify economic activity. On the other hand, a number of studies also strongly support the conclusion that arms expenditure is unsuitable as a means of engineering an economic boom, producing stability or creating employment.[16] The size of the armed forces and the extent of military research and development are largely decided in the long term. But instruments for effecting an economic boom mean possible short-term measures. When arms expenditure is to be used to promote structural change (in shipbuilding, for example) essential structural adaptations are often delayed, at the very least.

Moreover, the above-mentioned studies show clearly that the employment-promoting effect of state expenditure in the armaments sector is very much below the efficacy for the same purpose of capital investments in other areas of expenditure. That means that when arms expenditure is financed by increasing national expenditure as a whole, fewer additional jobs are created than if that expenditure were made in other areas.[17] If, indeed, the increased military expenditure is provided not by a higher national budget, but by manipulating budgetary items, that usually leads to a drop in the number of jobs. Therefore any positive effect of arms expenditure on unemployment is extremely questionable. It is a primary effect only when the finance is provided by increasing the national budget.

But then it is still not clear whether the requisite increase in national income would not lead elsewhere to a recession in employment, which would nullify that primary effect, say when finance is raised by increasing specific taxes. But even if there were a positive effect on the market, it would certainly be greater if expenditure occurred in other areas of application. Moreover, what I said in the last section remains true: arms expenditure is non-reproductive and cumulatively reduces the possibility of providing economic resources for other purposes in the future.

5. ARMAMENTS AND WELFARE

At first sight this statement seems quite clearly contrary to a principle of economics regarding the effects of national expenditure. It provides revenue irrespective of the utility of the means of provision, however meaningful the products or services obtained with its help. Galbraith made the direct link with armaments when he said that all honest political economists admitted that military requirements contributed a vast amount to the maintenance of our economic health. To be sure, arms expenditure also pays the workers and executives who produce the goods required in this sector, and then of course these people can spend their money privately. But that is true not only of arms expenditure but of all national expenditure. The production of idiotic, useless or potentially destructive and injurious things, however, even though the same effects on revenue may arise, does not result in an increase in total social welfare, but, as I have shown in the foregoing, means that the rise in social welfare remains below the level which it really could reach.[18]

We must also take into account the fact that the gross national product is a monetary yardstick of economic activity. It does not distinguish between advantage and injury afforded by the activity in question, above all in respect of the long-term consequences of this kind of economic management. At the same time we must remember that the rules for calculating the national product are no more than conventions of political economy. The first estimates of national revenue took into account only those goods and services which were designed for the market—and not military expenditure. Wittmann says in this regard:'The ruling notion was that this was expenditure to which no one could assign an advantage'.[19] How good it would be if this opinion of earlier statisticians were to prevail in practical politics.

Translated by J. G. Cumming

Notes

1. I am grateful to Bernhard Moltmann, Heidelberg, for numerous suggestions.
2. Stockholm International Peace Research Institute, Yearbook 1976, 231.
3. See also M. Kidron, R. Segal, *Die Armen und die Reichen* (Reinbek 1985) graph 7.
4. Cf. International Institute for Strategic Studies, The Military Balance 1985–1986 (London 1985) pp. 168–169.
5. Stockholm International Peace Research Institute: *Resources devoted to military research and development* (Stockholm, New York and London 1972) p. 3.
6. Cf. also Federal Minister for Defence (Ed.) *Weissbuch 1985: Zur Lage und Entwicklung der Bundeswehr* (Bonn 1985) p. 107.
7. This assumption seems paradoxical only at first sight, for if every country behaved in accordance with it, then all arms expenditure would be rendered void at one and the same time. But the expectations and behaviour of the other parties in each case are decisive, quite apart from the discussion whether the deflection by means of a pre-emptive strike of an attack expected directly should not be counted as defence in the broader sense.
8. P. A. Samuelson 'The Pure Theory of Public Expenditure'. *Review of Economics and Statistics*, Vol. 36, 1954, p. 387.
9. Cf. e.g., Klaus von Schubert *'Mutual Responsibility'—eine Strategie für West und Ost* (Heidelberg 1987), according to which it is time for an entirely new evaluation of the—economically expressed—level of goal attainment of arms expenditure for purposes of public security.
10. This is a view favourable to arms expenditure in so far as its basic assumption is that every additional expenditure involves an (even if marginal) positive increase in public security. Such an assumption excludes the question whether the piling up of constantly larger destructive potential also conceals a degree of potential danger (e.g.

68 ARMAMENTS AND POVERTY IN THE INDUSTRIAL NATIONS

storage of chemical weapons) or destabilisation (e.g. danger of a war started 'unintentionally' as the result of defective computers).

11. Cf. also J. Huffschmid, W. Voss and N. Zdrowomyslaw *Neue Rüstung—neue Armut* (Cologne 1986) pp. 54ff.

12. Ibid. p. 55.

13. J. Huffschmid *Rüstungs—oder Socialstaat* (Cologne 1981), documents a number of outstanding statements about this thesis (105f.).

14. Ibid. p. 1108.

15. Cf. H. Wulf, 'Die wirtschaftliche Bedeutung der Rüstungsindustrie in der BRd und Möglichkeiten der Umstellung auf zivile Produktion', E. Burhop and J. Huffschmid (Eds.) *Von der Kriegs—zur Friedensproduktion* (Cologne 1980) p. 81 Mary Kaldor terms arms technology 'baroque', since in the military sector extremely expensive maximum functional demands have to be made which in the civil sector are usually quite uneconomic: M. Kaldor, 'The Role of Arms in Capitalist Economies', D. Carlton and C. Schaerff (Eds.) *Arms Control and Technological Innovation* (London 1977) pp. 322ff.; also quoted in Huffschmid (1981) p. 109.

16. Cf. Huffschmid, Voss, Zdrowomyslav (1986) pp. 65ff. and the literature cited there.

17. Then national expenditure in other areas is (still) usually very seldom consciously used to promote employment.

18. Cf. also J. Huffschmid (1981) p. 115.

19. W. Wittmann *Der unbewältigte Wohlstand* (Munich 1972). On the development of social product calculation see T. Baumgartner, 'Wer was wie misst', Projektgruppe ökologische Wirtschaft (Eds.) *Arbeiten im Einklang mit der Natur* (Freiburg 1985) pp. 177ff.

Ignacio Ellacuría

Violence and Non-violence in the Struggle for Peace and Liberation

THE WORLD is full of all sorts of terrible violence: it is to be found on the personal, family, social, national and international levels. The problem of violence has unfathomable depths. If we look at armed conflicts alone, we find that the most developed powers consider that only the threat of the most terrible violence can protect them from actual violence: the balance of terror has taken the place of biological balance. But actual violence is widespread throughout the world: Iran-Iraq, Afghanistan, Kampuchea, Sri Lanka, India, Lebanon, Israel, South Africa, Angola, Nicaragua, El Salvador, Guatemala, Peru ... so many different places. There is also the so-called terrorist violence in Europe, particularly in Northern Ireland and the Basque Country.

From this complex mass of problems, I propose to take two examples of different forms of violence—one from the Third World: Latin America, and one from the First World: the Basque Country—because one needs to look closely at the statement that violence is wrong wherever it comes from. If by violence one means the unjust use of force, then it is always unacceptable. If by violence one understands the use of force pure and simple, then one at least has to say that some forms are worse than others, which leads one straight into the doctrine of the lesser evil. Comparing the revolutionary violence that has been used and is still being used in some countries in Latin America with the other sort of violence that is used in places in the First World, they will be seen to differ greatly from one another. Such a thorny problem does not lend itself to complete answers; one can only suggest lines of thought, first to those who are involved in violence, but also to those who study the problem from outside. We are all very much conditioned by what we see and live through. El

69

Salvador, from which I write, has known years and years of violence of various kinds. I will try to focus on the problem from there, while broadening out my remarks in space and time. Obviously each situation has its own historical antecedents that need to be borne in mind.

REVOLUTIONARY VIOLENCE IN LATIN AMERICA

The Medellín Conference of 1968, following the traditional teaching of the Church, most recently expressed by Paul VI in *Populorum progressio* (31), did not justify armed violence, but began to approach the problem of violence in a different manner. It pointed the way to the differentiation between levels and types of violence that was to be followed by liberation theology. It is a mistake to suppose that liberation theology encourages violence; one of its basic tenets is liberation *from* violence. What it has done is to analyse the social origin of violence and the overall means by which it can be overcome.

The original violence, the root and beginning of all other forms of violence in society, is what is called structural violence, which is simply structural injustice, the injustice of social structures, sanctioned by an unjust legal framework and an ideologically based cultural framework, which as such bring about the institutionalisation of injustice—institutional injustice. The unjust nature of structures and institutions has been pointed out by many people, inside and outside the Church for many years, but it took longer to see the violent nature of structures, of the economic order, of society, and the apparatus of the law. Yet an objective analysis of reality clearly shows the degree, predominance and extent of structural violence, which usually goes beyond what individuals intend, or groups realise is happening. The violence coupled with injustice of this structural-institutional violence can be seen by its results. When a society is structured in such a way that the bulk of its members are forced to live on a level of poverty so critical that the continuation of their physical lives is constantly threatened by lack of basic essentials, when they have to face up to hunger and sickness, have no access to basic education, work, housing, and so on, then such a society is both unjust and violent. It is unjust because it fails to respect what is most vital to every individual and most due to each; it is violent because it destroys life, because its structures and institutions make access to conditions necessary for survival impossible, obliging the majority—forcing them—to lead an inhuman life.

By the very nature of things, structural-institutional violence is accompanied by repressive violence. Continuous and systematic oppression through structures cannot be maintained in the long term, when it affects the greater part of the thinking population, except through various forms of repression. First it uses apparently non-violent means to keep the bulk of the people asleep and dreaming of fate or false expectations. When these means are no longer sufficient, harsher means are used, under the pretext that the security of the State—for which read the continuance of the unjust social order and political apparatus—is being endangered and that there is a Communist threat. Popular movements, even before they become armed uprisings, are hunted down and destroyed. The means used are legalised violence and what can truly be called terrorist violence. There is then state terrorism and the terrorism of the ruling classes, because their combined actions undertaken against defenceless people for the purpose or terrorising them into subjection, are terrorism. So at least forty thousand of those killed in El Salvador between 1980 and 1984 were victims of this combined state and class terrorism, whose joint instruments were the death squads.

These two types of violence—structural-institutional and repressive-terrorist—give rise to revolutionary violence. This appears in its purest form as an inevitable response to much greater evils and to a situation that precludes any other effective means of putting an end to a state of affairs that amounts not merely to a denial of political rights, but to a denial of life itself, through oppression and repression. Revolutionary-liberating violence in such a situation is an attempt to affirm the life that is being denied, to survive in the face of the rule of death, to free oneself from what prevents even minimal achievement of anything that might be called a human life. This revolutionary violence, when it has no other alternative, becomes armed struggle, without this implying that it is a terrorist struggle. It will adopt guerrilla tactics, which are by definition an irregular way of waging war, but are not the same thing as terrorist tactics. Terrorism is not something done by those who are first dubbed terrorists; those who carry out acts of terrorism, properly so-called, are the terrorists. The Sandinistas' struggle for liberation in Nicaragua, followed by their decision to abolish the death penalty after their triumph, shows what non-terrorist revolutionary violence can be, whatever mistakes they may have made. In theory, this form of revolutionary violence, in response to extreme cases of structural and terrorist violence, need not be seen as a form of class struggle nor be motivated by feelings of hatred and vengeance. It can be universal in character, representing the struggle of the oppressed and repressed against the structures of oppression and repression, stemming from identification with the poorest and aiming at the establishment of justice. Liberation struggles, whatever difficulties arise in their course, focus on the achievement of justice, but without losing sight of that other essential ingredient of peace: freedom. Liberation from structural injustice is aimed at making freedom really possible.

Nevertheless, whatever moral idealism inspires the revolutionary struggle, historical realism shows it to be an evil—though a lesser evil than the one it seeks to replace—and to bring major risks. First, it leads the opposing party to respond with even greater violence, thereby inflicting more suffering on the majority of the population. But also, the revolutionary struggle aimed at either achieving or retaining political and military power, in practice places the conquest or retention of such power in front of liberating the bulk of the people, this liberation being not so much a political one (liberation from repressive political power) as socio-economic (liberation from oppressive structures). When this happens, not only does the means (power) become the end, but the original main purpose is postponed indefinitely. There is also a danger of cloaking liberation from structural injustice and poverty in ideology, and nationalist ideology can be as dangerous as any other. There is also the problem of the way in which the revolutionary struggle for power is organised politically, not to mention the ideology used to interpret the struggle, which can lead to personal and group vengeance and hatred, which dehumanise and de-Christianise the idealistic potential of revolutionary struggle.

With all these attendant dangers, it is easy to condemn revolutionary violence in all cases. But such dangers, though they do form part of its reality, do not belong to the essence of revolutionary struggle. Of course armed conflict is always an evil, a greater evil than is often thought, and can only be allowed to be used when it will certainly avoid greater evils. But this evil is not to be measured according to a presumed abstract common good, which would make peace, understood simply as the absence of war, the supreme good, but from the standpoint of what provides a good necessary to the greatest number of the people. This good is, above all, satisfaction of their basic needs and effective respect for their basic human rights. It is just the negation of this necessary good that legitimises revolutionary violence, but this good then becomes the basic criterion of whether this violence should be used. To the extent that revolutionary struggle will foment, extend and consolidate this good, it is justified and even, up to a point, required; once it hinders the growth of this good, if not in the short term, but in the medium term, it then becomes unjustified in practice, despite its theoretical justification.

From an explicitly Christian standpoint, structural-institutional and repressive-terrorist violence are social sin by definition, being the fruit of sin, the embodiment of sin and the cause of a multitude of sins—particularly of the sin of making it impossible for the majority of the world's population to lead an even minimally human life. If God's original gift to humanity is life, then denying life is an actual denial of God in God's dealings with humanity. Any liberation process whose ends and means lead to overcoming this social sin is not only legitimate, but a positive part of the history of salvation.

Christian inspiration and historical experiences inspired by it point to the surmounting of violence, call insistently for the surmounting of social violence, by heroic means if need be and with the greatest possible identification with oppressed and repressed. This does not prevent Christians from having a clear vocation to peace, along with a holy, prophetic anger that will work itself out in action against the injustice done to the weakest. The first thing this calling to peace does is point out the ethical absurdity of seeking military solutions, backed by armaments sales, to conflicts between nations and social groups, especially in Third World countries that cannot afford to feed their people. So it points to a clear condemnation of the United States, which proposes a military and militaristic solution to the conflicts in Central America, one that can only be inimical to peace, now and in the future.

Applied to historical situations, this same Christian inspiration points to a preference for unarmed struggle against injustice. Revolutionary force does not necessarily and/or exclusively have to show itself in armed struggle. There are popular forms of struggle that have more to do with the social sphere than with political and military action. Prolonged social and political struggle, where the main agent is made up of the organised majority of the people engaged in active resistance and effective social pressure, without seeking to radicalise the situation and sharpen contradictions, but to end existing and imposed injustices, would seem to be more the sort of struggle that Christians should favour, even the most committed of them. Their aim would not be to seek reconciliation at any price—hence the fact that the struggle will be prolonged—but to avoid falling into the individual and group attitude that looks to armed struggle as the natural way to achieve political power, often of a totalitarian or near-totalitarian nature. If an armed struggle, aimed basically at liberation from structural injustice, is already in existence, then Christians can support it, provided that its pursuance offers a definite possibility of improvement in the material conditions of the majority within a reasonable space of time. Without such a possibility, negotiation would seem to be a better course to adopt. It is not arms that confer legitimacy, but arms can be a legitimate course, when they are taken up as a last resort to put an end to structural injustice.

Consideration of violence in a regional context should not leave out of account the responsibility of the First World in these matters. Many Third World countries have been victims of the violence of colonisation, from which they have liberated themselves through armed struggle. Now they are suffering the consequences of unjust terms of international trade and shameless political interference from the great powers, not to mention the lack of solidarity produced by consumerism, which opens up still greater gaps between rich and poor countries. All this leads to instability on a world-wide scale, places humanity in a state of violent tension and produces desperation rather than a quest for reasonable solutions. We are building up to a world-wide confrontation, not so much between power blocs, as between the great masses of people and the nations in which these masses are building up revolutionary pressure on the one hand—and the rich minorities and those nations that support them on the other. The great powers are responsible for the structural injustice of the world, which denies the majority of its inhabitants access to basic material needs and basic human rights. The great powers and their political alliances carry an enormous weight of responsibility for the violence in the world.

THE NONSENSE OF ARMED VIOLENCE IN THE FIRST WORLD

The problem of violence in the Third World, as we have seen, needs to be approached with a great deal of caution. Armed struggle, provided it does not take on terrorist forms, is justifiable; but only when structural injustice places a large part of the population in grave danger, either through depriving them of resources necessary for survival, or by repression that deprives those who fight for social justice of life itself. We now need to examine grounds adduced in support of revolutioary struggles in the First World.

At present the First World is not subject to military invasion or regimes of policy tyranny, though there do emerge forms of repression by police or other agencies. These conditions are not such as to warrant violent response, particularly when the ruling order is sufficiently democratic to allow other forms of struggle—unarmed and certainly without recourse to terrorism. There are, however, cases where a nation or culture feels itself dominated by another nation or culture within the context of a nation-state. These produce accusations of political or cultural genocide, through state power denying a historical people its rights to self-determination, or squeezing its language or culture to virtual extinction, leading to a call to set up an independent nation through armed struggle.

This is not the place to go into the inhumanity—potential and actual—involved in the concept of the nation-state, something that should now give way to a political order that takes account of the unity and universality of the human race. The specific case of the Basque Country shows that actions carried out by the nation-state can be based on pragmatic considerations: the integrity and unity of the nation-state are not in the category of absolute, but of historical value; so that it becomes debatable which popular will should historically decide how and in what area a people should find its identity. This involves points of principle which have real validity but which still need to be discussed. We need to see if we are really dealing with genocide of a people or a culture, which could be used as a justification for armed struggle.

Cultural genocide of a people, carried out on the basis of a more than political nationalism, is obviously a highly emotional subject that produces sharply antagonistic responses. Some people can only affirm their identity against others and tend to make themselves into victims in order to justify their diminished identity and lack of creative endeavour. They appeal to forced colonisation and imposition of an alien culture. This produces fanatical, revengeful and inhuman attitudes, in which individual irrationality prevents formation of a balanced overall view of reality. One might think this is what has happened in the Basque Country. On the one hand, there is forced erosion of the language, indigenous culture and national identity; on the other, a series of attitudes which, despite their positive idealism, fail to respond to reality—as can be seen not only from the fanatical discourse they employ, but from their recourse to strictly terrorist tactics. Taking the problem overall, there are three aspects with more general applications than to the Basque question alone.

The first is that the disappearance of certain forms of culture, and even of complete ways of life, is more dependent on *economic* than on political development. Once one accepts becoming a part of the dynamic of economic development, its inevitable demands bring about a deep change in one's cultural patterns. Ethnic culture has deep roots in immediate biological relationship with a particular environment and with reception of a past which has a profound influence on the less rational levels of individual and collective consciousness; yet it is nevertheless conditioned and even determined by the dynamics of economic and social development. So it would be more accurate to speak of the economic genocide of a people than its political genocide, which is largely self-destruction through acceptance of a particular economic system. This is what levels cultures, what favours some languages and customs rather than others—even if the cultural heritage maintains a degree of autonomy, taking on, interpreting and embracing the requirements of the economic structure and process in one way or another. Even if political self-determination is achieved, the problem of cultural genocide remains, since its principal determinant is the economic structure and not political will. This applies as much to capitalist economies as to socialist ones, as history has shown. This does not mean that we should undervalue the possibility of political self-determination on the part of those who share some common heritage; what it means is that this self-determination is political in nature and should be pursued through political means.

This brings us to the second question, which is that of *measured response*. If someone knocks out one of my teeth, I have no right to put out one of his eyes in self-defence. Physical life can only be taken when physical life is threatened.

In the case of revolutionary violence described in the first section, what is at stake is the preservation of the physical life of the vast majority, which justifies putting the physical lives of a minority at risk. But to place the physical lives of the majority at risk, especially when the majority are poor and needy, by pursuing objectives that go beyond protection of physical life, cannot be justifed. Some would hold that freedom, property, cultural identity and so on are more valuable than physical life, but life is the basic value that makes all others possible. In general, the principle of measured response suggests that cultural benefits should be achieved or defended by cultural means, political ones by political means, religious ones by religious means, and so on. Taking another person's life is in a different dimension from ethnic and cultural, class or political objectives, the more so when conditions exist in which these objectives can be achieved through proportionate means. It is often difficult to mobilise popular will effectively, but to replace this will by violent action carried out by a vanguard group speaking and deciding in the name of the people, is wrong and unjust. There are many forms struggle can take, and to opt for the most violent brings unacceptable consequences for those who suffer them and for those responsible for them.

The third consideration is the old maxim put forward to justify the use of violence, which is that is must be effective—must *succeed*. Since violence is an evil, its use can only be justified if it is going to achieve a good or at least the lessening of an evil. There could be no justification for violence that brings greater suffering to the majority. So it is entirely pertinent to ask how many deaths—in the extreme case of violence—or how many other quantifiable evils are going to be needed to achieve these or those—also quantifiable—goods. Until this equation has been set out and reasonably worked out, there can be no just recourse to violence. Prolonged popular resistance led by vanguard parties, the concept of the invincibility of a people in arms, the conviction that reason will always prevail, etc., do not measure up to the crude lessons of history.

Taking these three aspects into consideration, it would seem to be reasonable to state that certain types of violence have no justification in the First World. This certainly applies to all forms of terrorism, particularly those that bring death or destroy a person's physical or psychic integrity. Terrorism, defined as the use of—mainly physical—violence against defenceless people, civilians or otherwise, with the object of striking terror, is always reprehensible, the more so the greater the damage inflicted and the degree of defencelessness of the victim. But other forms of armed struggle are also unjustifiable, particularly when it has been shown that their continuance brings results disproportionate to their achievable objectives. This is a sphere in which ideological sophistry is rife, and there is a great need for critical discernment. If violence is the last resort, one has to exercise vision not to have too easy recourse to it and not to be carried away by the attraction armed struggle has for certain temperaments and certain age groups. Resorting to violence through lack of capacity to find other effective means is a confession of one's own limitations and a sure way to dehumanisation.

CONCLUSION

The foregoing remarks, dealing with the Third World and the First World, are reflections made from the standpoint of Christian faith, which points towards certain types of solutions—which also have their own justification, irrespective of what Christian faith has to say about them. Faith sees violence as intrinsically related to evil and explicable only in a world of sin, in which death generally prevails over life, egoism over altruism, vengeance over love, taking over giving. From a realistic point of view, acceptance of some forms of violence is inevitable, even for Christians, provided the principles and reservations set out above are taken into account, and provided these forms of violence are non-terrorist liberating violence, particularly that aimed at liberation from the death inflicted by institutionalised violence on the peoples of the Third World.

It would still seem that from the ultimate Christian standpoint, that of perfection in following the historical Jesus, those Christians who are Christian through and through in their attitudes and actions—while they will be the first and most heroic in fighting all forms of injustice—should not make use of violence. Not that Christians always and everywhere have to reject violence, but Christians acting as such will not normally give their specific witness through the use of violence. This does not mean they leave the 'dirty' work to others, counting themselves among the 'pure' who do not get their hands dirty. It is rather a question of giving the fullest and most comprehensive witness to the fact that life is above death, that love is stronger than hate. Such an approach will always be acceptable and effective, provided that these Christians are prepared to risk even martyrdom in their defence of the poor and struggle against the oppressors through the witness of their words and their life. There are different charisms in the Church, and different calls of the Spirit. With all due respect to each individual call, provided it is genuine, it does not seem either foolhardy or cowardly to state that the Christian calling is one to the use of peaceful means—which can be no less onerous—to the solution of the problem of injustice and violence in the world, rather than violent means, even though these can in some cases have justification.

Translated by Paul Burns

Edna McDonagh

Liberating Resistance and Kingdom Values

1. JUSTICE, FREEDOM AND PEACE

THAT MODERN political triad *liberty, equality and fraternity* has its parallel in the kingdom or reign of God as promised and promoted under both the Mosaic covenant and the 'new covenant in my blood' (Luke 22:30) which Jesus announced and inaugurated. Freedom, justice and peace are at once gifts and achievements of that saving presence and power of God called God's reign realised in Israel and in Jesus. They provide challenge and assurance to Christians today in their political struggles at a local level in First, Second or Third Worlds as well as in the more complex and universal struggles which derive from the intertwining of these worlds. The challenges have their immediate biblical resonances as we confront the disciple's call in the Sermon on the Mount to be justice-seeker and peace-maker (Matt. 5:6, 9) and the Pauline celebration of a Christian freedom which must combine with peace, build up rather than divide the community of Christ (cf. Eph. 2:14 etc.). Freedom, justice and peace remain for all the promise and the gift—as much aspiration as achievement in a sinful world. Christians are still and will always be in search of means to achieve and structures to express as effectively as possible that 'liberty, equality and fraternity' whose proclamation initiated the modern political world and whose biblical antecedents, despite much historical Christian neglect, are central to the Jewish-Christian promise and commitment. It is in the context of that promise and commitment that the right to resist and its forms will be considered here.

Given their close social and indeed kingdom connections, the denial of justice and freedom in any society involves the absence of true peace (cf. Jer. 6:14). Discrimination (refusal of what is due to certain groups of race, sex of class) and oppression (restricting the freedom of certain groups, all by a dominant group) create that state of unpeace, which is sometimes called 'institutional violence'. For its continuance, actual violence against the discriminated and oppressed by the security forces of the dominant is normal. Such situations exist in First and Third Worlds and *between* First and Third Worlds. Such situations call morally for the removal of discrimination and oppression, of the violence of the system, and the restoration of true peace with justice and freedom. A first step in that removal and restoration must be resistance. Christians for whom the kingdom values of justice, freedom and peace demand an expression in society, may not evade the call to *remove, restore and so resist.*

2. ARMED RESISTANCE IN CHRISTIAN HISTORY

Resistance as a Christian moral imperative in face of the anti-kingdom structures and practices prevalent *in* so many societies and *between* societies, must at the outset take account of the apparently contradictory imperatives proclaimed in that charter of God's new kingdom, the Sermon on the Mount. Scholarly sophistication, even if only occasionally lapsing into sophistry, does not readily domesticate the harsh demands 'Do not resist one who is evil ... love your enemies and pray for those who persecute you' (Matt. 5:45, 48). The only beloved Son of the Father, Jesus, lived this out in his own life, refusing to resist his enemies, accepting in love torture and death at their hands and with his last breath praying for forgiveness for them. It was such teaching and example that inspired Christians for three centuries to refuse military service and to seek to serve the good of the Roman Empire by the love, service and prayer which they had learned from their Master.

The access of Christians to political responsibility in the fourth century opened up new perspectives on the love and protection of the neighbour in society. Armed defence was gradually accepted as a necessary, if exceptional, expression of that love of neighbour. The first outlines of a justification of armed activity by Christians—of war, as indicated by Ambrose and Augustine and developed over the succeeding centuries—tried to contain such armed activity by its basic conditions: the cause of justice, defence of neighbour or punishment of persistent wrong-doers, undertaken by legitimate authority in very exceptional circumstances which offered no alternative. Even then the conduct of the war must respect certain basics, protection of innocent life as

Theodosius was forcibly told by Ambrose after the massacre at Thessalonica. This qualified acceptance of the use of armed force in society was discussed by St Thomas Aquinas under the virtue of charity and so distinct from his discussion of personal self-defence under the virtue of justice. For all the qualifications of the theologians and Church leaders, just-war theory, as it was subsequently called, was generally manipulated by the powerful to their own ends within the boundaries of their accepted jurisdiction and beyond. It was only with the change in the concept of sovereignty from its restriction to the monarch or prince and its extension to the people that moral resistance to the established powers was conceivable. The medieval reference to tyrannicide as justified in certain circumstances did of course in some slight way anticipate the justification of resistance and revolution which has emerged in the last two hundred years. However, it was secular politics and secular political philosophy which underpinned this moral justification. Churches and theologians only cautiously and ambiguously followed that secular lead. Today, however, the right to resist, and by force of arms if necessary, is widely discussed. Church and theological support for the political status quo may no longer be taken for granted in dozens of countries. What the Rhodesian (now Zimbabwean) bishops described in the 1970s as 'the demands of simple justice' are frequently invoked to justify resistance to the government and at times armed resistance. The location of sovereignty in the people rather than in the monarch, president or government has opened the way to delegitimising the current holder of office and the legitimacy of the people taking up arms to defend themselves in certain extreme circumstances. Just revolution has become an integral part of the theology of just war, with appropriate modifications in regard to the condition of 'declaration by the legitimate/competent authority'. From Negros to Soweto to San Salvador, the recourse to arms by an oppressed people in pursuit of justice, freedom and peace has received strong ecclesial and theological support. Yet the ambiguities persist. Ambiguities in describing the situation when President Aquino replaces President Marcos in the Philippines or when you distinguish between—if you do—the rebels in El Salvador and the Contras in Nicaragua; between any of them and the PLO, reaching on to such European phenomena as the IRA and the Red Brigade. The easy description of friends as freedom-fighters and of enemies as terrorists provides no moral guidance in trying to overcome the ambiguities. Invoking the traditional conditions of just cause, last resort, limited means, respect for non-combatants, etc., will lead different observers/participants to widely differing judgments. The history of such judgments by Church leaders and theologians, assessing the morality of their own state at war, is for the most part one of endorsement of their own civil authority at war with another external civil authority or with internal rebels.

3. RESISTANCE AND REVOLUTION TODAY

The acceptance in moral principle that armed revolution can be justified, analogous to other forms of just war, connects with other developments in the relations between church, society and state. In the First World there has been some perceptible move away from close identification with state-policies on defence and on justice issues at home and abroad by church leaders and theologians. Significant indicators of these moves have been the critical encyclicals by the US Catholic Bishops on 'Peace and War' and on the economy, and the Church of England's parallel working party reports, 'The Church and the Bomb' and 'Faith in the City'. The justice concerns of these economic documents do connect with the peace concerns of the others to enable the churches to approach their mission of proclaiming and promoting the advent of God's reign in society in a way that is independent and critical of the work of government. The Constantinian alliance and Theodosian establishment are being finally dismantled on the initiative of the churches themselves. In similar fashion the churches in Third World countries are taking on the task of promoting the kingdom values of justice and freedom in face of government oppression at home and economic oppression from abroad. The different emphases between First and Third World movements are important. First World preoccupation with 'peace' can seem a luxury to the oppressed in South Africa or Chile. Third World concentration on justice or freedom with the risk of violent upheaval can appear very threatening to First World church leaders. Yet in a diminishing world, the global interconnection of the kingdom triad of justice, freedom and peace offers an urgent challenge to the kingdom-discerners and kingdom-promoters called Christians, around the world. The struggle for justice and freedom in Third World countries is an integral part of the First World's search for peace. Resistance to injustice and unfreedom in South Africa for example, must be on the agenda of Christian peace-activists in Europe.

The structures and practices of injustice, oppression and violent destruction which take a specific and concentrated form in any particular country are part of a global pattern. The complete overcoming of such anti-kingdom structures and activities demands finally a global transformation. Such complete and global change is for Christians eschatological—to be discerned, striven for and anticipated now. In its completeness it constitutes the completion of history. The struggle here and now is both particular and global. The pattern to be reversed has its particularities in every particular country but also its universalities which challenge a wider, connecting world.

The emergence of any new just, liberating and constructive pattern involves the two moments of negation and creation: of resistance to the destructive patterns and creation of the constructive. The task of resistance into new creation is one which Christians share with all people of good will but to which they also bring their own particular insights and strengths. These will no doubt always have a shadow-side as the historical blindness and weakness of Christians shows.

4. KINGDOM PRESUMPTIONS AND RESISTANCE TO OPPRESSION

The promise and proleptic realisation of the reign of God in justice, freedom and peace specifies the anticipatory consciousness (Bloch) which fuels the political struggles of humanity. Promise and realisation, however faint, provide a presumption of justice/equality, freedom/liberty and peace/fraternity/solidarity by which Christians and people of good will may evaluate and respond to a particular political situation. In face of injustice, inequality and discrimination Christians at least must act on this God-given, Christ-founded (cf. Gal. 3:58) presumption that justice and equality shall prevail. In a taken-for-granted way they condemn and seek to remove the practices and structures of injustice and assume the political conversion in attitude of those who maintain the practices and structures. In pursuit of these changes they use whatever political and social means are available in publicity and persuasion, in organisation and party, in election and parliament. Where these changes are resisted by the maintenance people through simple refusal or dishonest stalling, counter-resistance of a more urgent and coercive kind is required. This may, and frequently will, expose the deeper resistance of the oppressing group in their use of armed and physical destructiveness against the leaders and supporters of the promoters of justice and freedom. The injustice and oppression assume a more overtly and physically violent form. Peace becomes as clearly violated as justice and freedom. The full dimensions of the counter-kingdom character of the regime are gradually revealed. The challenge to the justice-seekers, freedom-forgers and peace-makers committed to the reign of God becomes more acute. What form shall their further response take? shall they meet physical violence with counter-violence? Shall they abandon the struggle and await conversion of heart rather than adopt the violent means of their oppressors? Have they other options?

Before attempting to answer these questions it may be worth considering more fully the schematic outline developed here on the basis of a presumption of kingdom values. Such a presumption offers a different starting-point from the more traditional presumption of the validity and inevitability of the political and economic status quo, however unjust and oppressive. With this new presumption, the oppressed may morally assert—indeed assume—their rights. Resistance to right is then clearly seen to be located in the maintenance of the unjust and unfree status quo. It is from there in pursuing the resistance to right that the originating and immoral violence emanates. The assumption and active assertion of kingdom values by the oppressed and their allies is, of course, both morally right and morally obligatory. Their resistance to further oppression and its physically violent accompaniment shares the same moral status. Such resistance for the kingdom and on behalf of the oppressed community of neighbours is not opposed to the Sermon on the Mount. Simple resignation is a denial of the kindgom presumption and a refusal of the kingdom call.

The kingdom presumption and call apply to all in a particular political and economic society. Given the global interconnection of contemporary societies and the global range of the kingdom, presumption and call extend beyond any particular society to involve, for example, people in First and Third Worlds in regard to particular issues, as indicated earlier. What needs to be emphasised just here is how kingdom presumption and call apply to those who maintain the benefit from injustice and oppression in a particular society. Their 'privileged' deafness and blindness are in need of removal not merely for the sake of the oppressed but for their own sakes, that they may be enabled to enter the kingdom both in its anticipatory and final stages.

The kingdom with its camel and eye-of-the-needle difficulty for wealthy oppressors is not to be finally barred to them, if they cease oppressing, become converted and, with their oppressed neighbours, cooperate in establishing kingdom values of justice, freedom and peace. The inclusivity of the kingdom is directed towards embracing repentant and reconciled oppressors. Along this line one can see how love of enemies requiring their conversion and inclusion in the kingdom also requires the assumption and assertion of kingdom values by the oppressed and their allies. The true liberation of the oppressed is the only mode of true liberation for the oppressor, enslaved by his privileges and powers and so excluded from the company of the poor and powerless sinner-saints who enjoy the kingdom-fellowship of Jesus. Resistance to oppression and transformation of oppressive structures, activities and attitudes is as much a matter of saving-liberating importance for the powerful and privileged as for the powerless and deprived. 'Love of enemies' and 'turning the other cheek' may, for the sake of the enemy as well as the neighbour, demand loving but firm resistance.

5. PRIORITY OF THE DEPRIVED

Yet the priority lies with the deprived. It is their assumption and enjoyment of kingdom values which provide both test and way of the developing reign of God in history. From them and with them comes the saving and liberating impulse of the Spirit. Wherever they are there is the power and call of the Spirit to which the rest of us must answer. The 'upside-down' nature of the kingdom is fully revealed in seeking divine presence, power and call where human power and presence seem deprived and defaced to the point of near obliteration. Solidarity with the victims in opposition to victimisation is a concrete kingdom command, deriving eventually from Calvary, where the call and the power to end victimisation were finally proclaimed. Resistance to continuing victimisation in its myriad forms constitutes a primary Christian vocation. Strategies for such resistance demand today a new exercise in Christian commitment and imagination as the victimisation becomes more penetrating, devious and disguised and the need for an inclusive, kingdom-based society more urgent and in some ways more feasible.

6. POLITICAL AND ECONOMIC STRATEGIES OF RESISTANCE

Strategies based on kingdom presumptions must provide effective protection to the immediately and most destructively victimised. They must provide a way forward by preventing activities of oppression, dismantling its structures and finally—usually finally—converting the oppressors. Over two hundred years a range of strategies for overcoming victimisation has developed. Political organisation and pressure of the kind pioneered at least on a grand scale by Daniel O'Connell in Ireland in the early nineteenth century, continue to be effective in many situations. They need international publicity and support if they are not to be ignored or lead to even greater oppression in arbitrary arrest, detention and torture of leaders or still more violent response against unarmed protesters. Hungary (1956) and Sharpeville (1960) and Bull Connors (Alabama 1963) and a host of other places and people give eloquent testimony to the violent resistance of the establishment to the legitimate political activities of the oppressed.

Economic sanctions have an important role to play. The 'boycott' devised in Ireland late in the nineteenth century can be another effective vehicle for radical social change. The weakness of First World countries in applying economic sanctions in support of the oppressed in the Third World and the crocodile tears of their leaders of how the sanctions might damage the oppressed rather than assist them, are particularly painful examples of our failure to promote serious alternatives to armed counter-violence as the only response to oppression.

7. ARMED COUNTER-VIOLENCE

Given the traditional theology of 'just war' armed counter-violence by the victims could clearly be justified in certain extreme circumstances. Indeed, there is quite a strong case for saying that only such a revolution might satisfy the criteria of just war theology. This is based on the availability of alternatives in the case of international disputes and the destructive potential of international warfare; while a war of revolution—confined to a particular society suffering from tyrannical oppression without any other prospect of removing it—might well satisfy the traditional criteria.

Such a judgment may not, of course, be readily made. For those who accept just war theology it may not be in principle excluded. And it clearly must be the judgment of people inside the oppressive situation, firmly committed to and engaged in overcoming the oppression by all other available means and reluctant to adopt the violent means of their opponents. With this kingdom engagement and mentality they have at least theological precedent for seeking to restrain the oppressor and overcome the oppression by force of arms.

8. HISTORICAL AMBIGUITIES AND KINGDOM VISION

Force of arms in defence of the victims has long been part of the Christian tradition. That does not immediately dissolve the difficulties it creates for kingdom-seekers. The inclusivity of the kingdom to which the love of enemies directly refers, the repentance of oppressors and reconciliation with oppressed which that implies, underlines the kingdom vision of equality, liberty and solidarity which transcends traditional divisions of Jew and Gentile, slave and free, male and female. Such a vision, with its required if only partial realisation in history, institutes a presumption against the historical elimination of the oppressor-enemy. The way of Christian resistance to oppression finds it easier to justify dying for the other (oppressed) than to justify killing the other (oppressor). The more profound kingdom call seeks ways to achieve justice and freedom in solidarity and peace with an oppressor freed from his oppressing attitudes and activities. A First World Christian contemplating oppression in the Third World will be urgently seeking ways to help Third World Christians to achieve this anticipation of kingdom values without recourse to the destructiveness of armed force. A Third World Christian in turn will be looking for ways within that situation to act on the kingdom-presumption without recourse to the destructive, violent means of the oppressor. This was central to the strategies of resistance devised by Gandhi and Martin Luther King. Third World Christians are also helped by First

World examples in overcoming its own more moderate internal oppression and First World support in overcoming the widespread political and economic engagement of First World countries with oppression in the Third World. The fuller Christian way of resistance into an inclusive kingdom depends very much on the conversion of First World Christians to the concrete demands of justice and freedom and solidarity.

PART III

Painful Pressure Points as Stimuli for New Thinking

G. Clarke Chapman, Jr.

Theology of Deterrence and Nuclearism

IF IT is true that nuclear weapons pose the greatest threat ever to civilisation and to global life, why do humans rarely seem able to sit down and think clearly about the danger? An answer must be sought at two levels. The easy reply is that since 1945 no world war has erupted among the super-powers, it would appear that nuclear deterrence has preserved the uneasy peace. So earlier anxieties of Doomsday have receded. However, there is a deeper answer, I believe, which is now coming to light. A powerful covert religion, 'nuclearism', has so dominated our public psyche that the gravitational pull of its mythic imagery gravely distorts our perception of danger.

NUCLEARISM AS A RELIGION

The term nuclearism has been popularised by Robert Jay Lifton, a Yale psychiatrist who pioneered in the study of Hiroshima survivors. Modern societies, he notes, have seen the degeneration of vital symbols of the continuity of life. Hence nuclearism offers 'the passionate embrace of nuclear weapons as a solution to death anxiety and a way of restoring a lost sense of immortality'.[1] Any religion is devoted to life in its totality, as well as its ultimacy, and in the secret recesses of the public consciousness 'the Bomb' seems to satisfy both these functional criteria. For early witnesses describing nuclear tests, their experience of numinous awe drove them to use sacred imagery of divine judgment, wrath, or a newborn world. For the rest of us, moreover, the Bomb continues to evoke powerfully religious sensations: fear yet fascination, mortal vulnerability to invisible cosmic forces, a sense of mystery and nemesis in the presence of seemingly infinite power.

Lifton offers clinical descriptions of the disruptive effects of nuclearism on the psyche. Failing to cope rationally with the Bomb, the mind instead responds in two discordant ways. A pyrotechnic barrage of fragmentary images dazzles and preoccupies us, prompting those restless experimentations in lifestyle and quests for personal identity so typical of our times. But simultaneously we are burdened by 'psychic numbing', a chronic depression and apathy such as survivors of concentration camps and other disasters have experienced. Haunted by the unthinkable, the mind protectively shuts down. This is evidenced by such psychic mechanisms as denial of obvious experience, and euphemisms about the grotesque—'Nuke-speak', for instance, about nuclear 'exchanges', population 'relocation', and 'Peacekeeper' missiles.

Recently Lifton's research has attracted attention from North American religious scholars. Using history-of-religions methodology, Ira Chernus is a pioneer in analysing the mythic dimensions of public perceptions of the Bomb.[2] Some theologians also are beginning to address nuclear weapons as representing something beyond one more *ethical* dilemma, i.e., 'problems' requiring new strategies and accountability but still presuming the competency of human problem-solvers. Instead these weapons are emerging as a *theological* issue, a challenge to fundamental concepts of God, the creation, and humanity.[3] This demands an unprecedented new seriousness from theology.

Indeed, if nuclearism be an alternative religion, it ought also to be called 'heresy'. Against this, only a confessional response can suffice. Let us pray that God even now is preparing a new Reformation, a birthing time when the Spirit once again will guide the churches to reclaim their identity through 'a special case for confessing'. The time has not yet come when nuclearism is widely acknowledged as a false faith. But there is ample precedent in twentieth-century stands against Nazism and apartheid for the churches now to strive toward a *status confessionis* declaration against the Bomb. However, this should include more than official pronouncements; we must work at the grass roots level for new ways of thinking and living—ways which will render nuclearism less credible, while opening hearts for renewal.[4]

DETERRENCE AS AN IDEOLOGY

Let us return now to the simpler, more popular explanation of the puzzling absence of clear thinking about the nuclear threat. Is it true that strategic deterrence has thus far prevented World War III? Or might it be instead that a fortunate but temporary stability in geopolitical balance has bestowed on that doctrine an illusion of efficacy? Certainly if we wish to plumb the depths of nuclearism, we must also analyse this, its most prestigious doctrine. Can deterrence withstand careful scrutiny? Or is it largely an ideology serving to mask darker human urges?

An official definition of deterrence is '*the prevention from action by fear of the consequences. Deterrence is a state of mind brought about by the existence of a credible threat of unacceptable counter action.*'[5] But any language about 'states of mind' induced by 'credible' action is already religious language! The whole construct rests on faith judgments. Whether or not deterrence even *exists* is a matter which can be known only by a potential aggressor. Indeed, comments one observer, 'Strategic analysis is a dream world. It is the realm of data-free analysis. There is no test data, no combat data'. When anticipated attacks do not occur, no cause for such 'non-events' can ever be demonstrated. The very concept of deterrence has been called 'a gift to strategists in that its nature and workings remain so elusive and so imperfectly understood as to permit endless speculation with little danger of empirical refutation, and justifying the maintenance of almost any military capability on the grounds that it might be doing good and we could well be worse off without it'.[7]

The notion of averting unwanted behaviour by timely threats, however, is an everyday experience lending plausibility to the strategic doctrine. The average person wants to believe that demonstrations of strength are effective. Deterrence evokes comforting images of a nuclear umbrella—with emotional overtones of safety and protection which go far beyond its conceptual substance. This instrinsic ambiguity has been further compounded recently by the strategies of 'flexible response', 'counterforce', or 'nuclear war fighting' (and even 'prevailing'). As rash novelties, they all nevertheless aspire to squeeze under the earlier label—e.g., as 'extended deterrence'. Consequently 'nuclear deterrence today means whatever the speaker wishes it to mean. It is a blank cheque'.[8] Perhaps the umbrella metaphor, now stretched beyond recognition, should be replaced by this blank cheque image—or, merging the two, a seriously overextended, 'bounced' cheque!

DETERRENCE: A SECULAR CRITIQUE

The doctrine of deterrence has been faulted on various non-theological grounds by many social scientists. Patrick Morgan, for instance, criticises its abstractness, a formalism which neglects the factual—overlooking the dynamics of what actually may cause war or how governments make decisions. His writings offer an excellent survey of relevant social science data.[9] There are quite disparate situations of deterrence, for example, which ought not be conflated; those threats that mollify one set of circumstances may only aggravate another. Discrimination is needed to judge which actions might best influence a particular antagonist. There are many models of government decision-making, and each yields differing notions of deterrence. Even clear threats may be misjudged, due to the bureaucratic pressures of 'groupthink' or overconfidence in crisis management. And misperceptions are even more likely in the volatile atmosphere generated by emergencies.

Additional problems with deterrence have been widely noted.[10] 1. By waiting to react to an adversary's initiative, one's weapons lose their political value to coerce. 2. To be credible a threat aspires to be unambiguous—but to that degree also forfeits the flexibility required by statecraft. 3. There is a moral repugnance to planning mass murder of civilians, the hostages of the nuclear age. 4. For these reasons, deterrence violates the traditional honour of the military profession and tends to undermine morale for leaders and citizens alike. 5. Because of advancing technology, deterrence is forever unstable; there can never be 'enough' really to guarantee an invulnerable retaliation to pre-emptive attack. 6. Nor can we rely on deterrence to work indefinitely, outrunning the eventual probability of catastrophic accident or human error.

DETERRENCE: A THEOLOGICAL CRITIQUE

But it is especially at the theological level that this ideological cover for nuclearism must be refuted. 'Nuclear deterrence, after all, is a quasi-theology. It has a dogmatic character and an elaborate theoretic superstructure. It is prone to absolute claims about the deepest springs of human motivation and conduct—although, like too many churchly theologies, nuclear deterrence lacks a fully rounded view of human experience.'[11]

The root of its error, therefore, is its distorted model of human nature: an unstable compound of both rationalist and bestial extremes. This bifurcated anthropology is a grotesque parody of the Christian vision of humanity as simultaneously *imago Dei* and fallen creature. 'If deterrence theorists' absolute presumption of rationality seems to exalt cerebral powers to superhuman levels, their punitive preoccupation with threats seems to degrade *homo sapiens* to subhuman levels.'[12] Accordingly these theorists propose first 'that we should frustrate our opponents by frightening them very badly and that we should then rely on their cool-headed rationality for our survival.'[13]

THE HUMAN AS MANAGER

On the one hand, according to deterrence doctrine, the *imago Dei* is flattened into a shallow, technocratic rationalism. National leaders are elevated to supreme crisis managers toying with primal forces of the cosmos and yet confident of skirting the abyss. This misplaced trust in rationality gains plausibility in our high-tech society which clings to the premise that persons are self-contained monads, sublimely logical and detached from other selves. By taking command of oneself, the managerial mentality fancies itself entitled to a wider right of domination—whether in exploiting nature or manipulating people.

Recent theories of 'nuclear warfighting' carry this self-confidence to horrifying extremes. But from the beginning of the nuclear era, it has always been problematical to find a rational basis for using the Bomb. At such magnitudes of destruction, it may well be irrational to retaliate if attacked; yet such an admission would undermine the very credibility on which deterrence rests. Thus the dilemmas of unprecedented power expose the self-contradictions of rationalism. Furthermore, it is theologically incompatible with biblical anthropology. In Scripture the 'XIX' is certainly not posited as a self-sufficient monad, but as a complex bundle of opposites, finite yet free, whose selfhood is attained only in reciprocity with other selves and the divine Thou.

THE HUMAN AS BEAST

On the other hand, deterrence caricatures the fallenness of humanity—to such an extreme as to warrant the threat of final terror. Abruptly, like the plunge of a roller coaster, the portrayal of human nature plummets now to a bestial level. Persons are considered subhuman creatures who must be frightened into decent behaviour. Ever since the crossbow, history has witnessed a search for the ultimate weapon which would somehow impose 'peace'. An example is Alfred Nobel, famed inventor of dynamite: 'I wish I could produce a substance or invent a machine of such frightful efficiency for wholesale destruction that wars should thereby become altogether impossible'.[14]

Apparently the goal is to scare people into rationality—or at least into seeing things our way! But the logic of terror is internally inconsistent and self-defeating. Fear does not produce clarity but confusion, and impending catastrophe is a poor learning atmosphere for teaching the recalcitrant 'a lesson'. To the contrary, Lifton and other psycho-analysts observe, once a certain anxiety threshold is passed, the mind shuts down or reverts to childish fantasy.

Moreover, the degradation of human nature to subhuman levels by threat is just as theologically objectionable as in the inflation of humanity to omnicompetence. Intimidation degrades both the user and the recipient. The latter is satisfyingly demonised into 'the Enemy', upon which all our own unacceptable qualities are then projected and vilified.

By contrast, Jesus' parable of the Good Samaritan (Luke 10:29–37) replaces the easy 'Enemy' reflex with the uncomfortable question, 'Who is my neighbour?' Salvation is near when we can acknowledge a part of ourselves to exist in 'them', thus on both levels enabling us to reach out and embrace the alienated. Mutuality among the components of the self, as well as reciprocity with other selves, are gifts from God. Both are rooted in God's gracious covenant and reach fulfilment in God's promised reign. It is by this vision that the theological shortcomings of deterrence must be measured and the deeper heresy of nuclearism contested. This is the vision which calls us now to a new confession of faith.

Notes

1. Lifton *The Broken Connection* (New York 1979) p. 369.
2. See Chernus *Dr. Strangegod: On the Symbolic Meaning of Nuclear Weapons* (Columbia 1986).
3. *E.g.*, see Gordon D. Kaufman *Theology for a Nuclear Age* (Philadelphia 1985); Dale Aukerman *Darkening Valley* (New York 1981).
4. See my book *Facing the Nuclear Heresy* (Elgin 1986).
5. JCS Pub. 1, quoted by *The Defense Monitor*, 12:3 (June 1983) p. 5.
6. Pierre Sprey, quoted by Fred M. Kaplan *Dubious Specter* (Washington D.C. 1980) p. 41.
7. Lawrence Freedman, quoted by Alan Geyer *The Idea of Disarmament!* (Elgin 1982) p. 36.
8. K. D. Johnson 'The Morality of Nuclear Deterrence' in *The Nuclear Crisis Reader* ed. Gwyn Prine (New York 1985) p. 145.
9. Patrick M. Morgan *Deterrence* (Beverly Hills 1977) and 'New Directions in Deterrence Theory' in *Nuclear Weapons and the Future of Humanity* eds. Avner Cohen and Steven Lee (Totowa 1986) pp. 169–89.
10. *E.g.*, see Allan Kraes 'Deterrence and Its Contradictions' in *Toward Nuclear Disarmament and Global Security* ed. Burne H. Weston (Boulder 1984) pp. 211–14.
11. Greyer, *op. cit.* p. 192.
12. *Ibid.* p. 55.
13. Karl Deutsch, quoted in *ibid.* p. 53.
14. Nobel, quoted by Morgan *Deterrence* p. 107.

Joachim Garstecki

Marxist Teaching on the Just War

WAR AS A PHENOMENON OF THE CLASS SOCIETY

THE MARXIST-LENINIST teaching on war and peace demands, for the first time in the history of mankind, that a consistent connection be made between the scholarly analysis, and the moral assessment, of war and peace. The question as to whether a war is morally just or unjust remains unanswerable, according to the Marxist view, until it is connected with a thorough theoretical and philosophical definition of war as a symptom of the class society. The basis for this definition lies in the Marxist philosophy of history. Here, a criterion is introduced for classifying a war as 'just' or 'unjust': whether or not the war is in sympathy 'with the needs and objective demands of the development of mankind'[1] and these demands are claimed as known. The decisive turning point of the Marxist-Leninist 'teaching on the just war' is to understand the function of war within the 'objective' process of history, and its interpretation in each respective age.

Accordingly, there is no original connection between the Marxist teaching on war and the Christian tradition of the just war. The characteristics of the *justum bellum* developed by Christian ethics are considered by Marxists to be incapable of revealing the true interests of the states involved in a war. Christian moral teaching has not been able to produce any substantive criteria as to the sort of denial of rights which necessitates war and thus what cause of war is considered just. Neither did the bourgeois Enlightenment go beyond a moral proscription of war; it simply saw peace as a moral postulate following from an abstract notion of the 'nature of man'. In Marxism on the other hand, the Christian and bourgeois judgments about the justification of war are 'inherited' in that, true to materialism, they are turned 'head over heels'. Marx, Engels—and particularly Lenin who is the standard interpreter of Marxism in the 20th century—relate the legal and moral legitimacy of wars strictly to their class content. The 'legitimacy and legality' of a war are to be judged "from the standpoint of the social proletariat and its fight for liberty; we recognise no other standpoint".[2] The assessment of a war as "just" or "unjust" requires analysis of the policies which are continued by the war. For war is nothing other than 'a simple continuation of politics by other methods'[3]—by the methods of military strength.

REVOLUTION AND WAR AS MEANS TO PEACE

It is no coincidence that the Marxist-Leninist teaching on war is placed by its theoreticians within the framework of a 'philosophy of peace'. The historical mission of the working class consists of overcoming the evil of the class society and bringing in the reign of peace through a classless society. The roots of this missionary project extend far back beyond Marx. They are based on the Enlightenment idea of eternal peace which conceives of wars as the consequence of the socialisation of mankind. With the transition to capitalist methods of production, bourgeois society and its constitutive principle of private property is identified as the cause of war. The 'war of classes'[4] is the true obstacle on the path to peace for mankind. The revolutionary social impetus of the nineteenth century, to eradicate the pauperisation of the working masses in a final violent act, a revolutionary civil war, becomes the centre of the Marxist theory of history. 'With the abolition of class domination, war disappears as well. The fall of capitalism means world peace.'[5]

In contrast to this, the later writings of Engels actually consider civil war to be avoidable.[6] The working class as the subject of social progress ought not to come to power through war but through political revolutions. The classical Marxist-Leninist thinkers do not justify war as such, but they see in it a historically necessary means to the end of achieving a better peace. The amount of military power is dependent on the concrete historical and political circumstances; a systematic reflection about the suitability of the means is not part of classical Marxism.

After the Russian Revolution in 1917, Lenin's theoretical interests turned away from revolution and reverted more strongly to war. Economic social analysis was replaced by the legal and moral assessment of military power.

This is the expression of an expectation of world revolution which is still only ideologically held and which had certainly not appeared after the victory of the October revolution in Russia. The socialist order which had lately arisen had to establish itself—against predictions of Marx—in the ongoing original circumstances and defend itself against counter-revolution. The Leninist teaching on war is a necessary consequence of the 'Parousia delay' of the world revolution; it corresponds in political terms to the principle of 'peaceful coexistence'.

The classification of the relationship between revolution and war, after 1945, became significant for the Marxist on revolutionary wars of liberation. A 'correct understanding of the perspectives of the revolutionary world process, of the complicated and contradictory mutual relationship between war and social progress, between war and revolution'[7] is considered especially important. Behind this dialectical statement the recognition is beginning to dawn that the military methods of war have the tendency to destroy its revolutionary aims. Lenin said, 'Revolution is war',[8] but the 'spilling over' of a revolution into war could nowadays release a catastrophe, destroying everything. In certain circumstances a peaceful transition from capitalism to socialism might be considered possible.

WAR CEASES TO BE A CONTINUATION OF POLITICS BY OTHER METHODS

The Marxist-Leninist doctrine states that weapons and wars will accompany mankind until socialism wins a world-wide victory. On the other hand, the working class can only fulfil its peace mission if its revolutions are capable of defending themselves. In the current interpretation of this doctrine, however, there have always been modifications; such modifications have at present a strong retroactive effect on the self analysis of the Marxist-Leninist teaching on war and they make the provision of reliable statements about the state of discussions and possible developments difficult. In contrast to the original formulation of the unavoidability of war, there arose, after the 20th party conference of the KPdSU in 1956, the concept of a third world war being avoidable on account of the increased strength of the socialist position. The danger of an atomic war in which there would be no winners, only losers, gives rise nowadays to the demand to avoid an atomic war at all costs. An atomic war is 'objectively' no longer suitable for the continuation of politics. Its means and methods have extended beyond all conceivable aims of war. If war loses its function of being a continuation of politics using the means of power, it also loses its capability of 'being transformed into socialist revolution, into social progress.'[9] The aim of communism is therefore tied to preventing war.

The prevention of war is thus itself social progress and at the same time the 'condition of social progress'.[10] War has become obsolete even before the complete disappearance of its social origins.

The political consequences of this theoretical realisation are summarised in the Soviet Union in the programmatic leitmotif 'New thinking in the Atomic Age'.[11] The political logic of the nuclear age 'must be understood as quickly as possible'; this necessitates 'testing whether the traditional political ideas in the strictly delineated area dealing with war and peace—that is to say, with the existence of mankind—are still adequate for their subject matter'.[12] The 'new thinking' also makes the theoretical axioms of Marxist-Leninist doctrine on war and peace subject again to the criterion of the practical.[13] 'Today's world is much too small and fragile for wars and the politics of strength. It cannot be saved and maintained if we do not break decisively and finally with the way of thinking and acting which has for centuries been based on the justifiability and acceptability of wars and armed conflicts.'[14]

In the wake of such re-thinking, the Leninist principle of peaceful coexistence among states of differing social orders also gains new content. Before, it was primarily interpreted as the ideological form of the class conflict; now it has become a minimum condition for a cooperative peace between the two world systems. Peaceful coexistence can no longer be a means of changing capitalism into socialism. Rather, they must both accept the necessity of agreements which will make them equal partners in securing peace and in the competition between societies. 'The basic recognition on both sides of the possibility of peace in a dialogue between systems' is offered, although this does not yet imply 'any consequence to be drawn about the concrete readiness for peace.'[15] On this basis, security can be organised as common security.[16]

THEORY, POLITICS AND UNIVERSAL HUMAN ETHICS

It remains for the time being an open question how disadvantageous the effect of the economic and political realism of the 'new thinking' is for Marxist-Leninist theory about war and peace and how it changes it. Each socialist policy is under a certain amount of pressure to justify itself over against the actual ideology. This is particularly true of defence policies. Marxist military theorists try to demonstrate that 'new thinking in the atomic age' represents a logical development from the traditional understanding of the nature of war and peace.[17] Thanks to a considerable straining of the concept, this is not difficult to demonstrate—given that we follow the inner logic of the Marxist-Leninist thought structure. The atomic age cannot overcome the social and political antagonism of the systems, but rather makes it more radical because it becomes unmistakeably clear which policy promotes peace and which does not. It remains true that a war to defend socialism with atomic weapons would be morally just if it had to be waged[18]—but this is to word the question wrongly. A just defensive war will become superfluous when the necessity to wage it becomes superfluous. The key to this is the dismantling of military confrontation between west and east, disarmament and the renouncement of all attempts to gain military superiority. The pressure to act produced by the will to survive affects the Marxist doctrine of war more strongly nowadays than the theory of class conflict affects politics. This is required by the theoreticians' openness to learning. They see it as important that the peaceful coexistence which at present is still an armed peace can and should develop towards becoming a peace without arms.[19] The socialist rhetoric on the subject of peace is audible here. The powers with atomic weapons must 'stop separating politics from the universal human ethical norms'.[20]

The universal human ethical norms are not yet a determining factor. The nuclear threat does not yet constitute the one common subject for a united humanity capable of leaving behind all particular justifications of deterrents, defence and 'just' war. But politics has begun to leave the ivory tower of such justifications.

Translated by Jane Curran

Notes

1. G. KieBling, W. Scheler 'Friedenskampf und politisch-moralische Wertung des Krieges' in *Dt. Ztschr. f. Phil.* 24 (1976) 1, p. 44.
2. W. I. Lenin *Werke* Vol. 27 (Berlin⁵ 1978) p. 324.
3. C. V. Clausewitz *Vom Kriege* (Berlin 1957) I p. 34.
4. K. Marx, letter to F. Engels, 28.7.1870 in *MEW* 33 (Berlin 1966) p. 12.
5. Congress of the 2nd Internationale, Zürich 1893, *Protokoll of the Intern. Soz. Arbeiterkongresses*, Zürich August 1893 (Zürich 1894) p. 20.
6. F. Engels Introduction to 'Der Bürgerkrieg in Frankreich 1895' in *MEW* 22 (Berlin 1962) p. 521ff.
7. *Die marxistische-leninistische Lehre von Krieg und Armee* (Berlin 1986)— *Marxistko-Leninskoe uschenije o vojne i armii* (Moskau 1984) ed. D. A. Wolkogonow p. 78.
8. W. I. Lenin *Werke* vol. 8 (Berlin⁵ 1984) p. 95.
9. K. Hager 'Marxismus-Leninismus und Gegenwart'. Lecture at the Humboldt University in Berlin on 24.10.1986. (Berlin 1986) p. 14.

10. K. Hager *ibid.* p. 16.

11. See A. Gromyko, W. Lomejko *Neues Denken im Atomzeitalter* (Berlin 1985)—*Novoe myslenie v adernyi vek* (Moskau 1984).

12. G. CH. Schachnasarow 'Die politische Logik des Nuklear-zeitalters' in *Sowjetwissenschaft*/Ges. Beiträge (1984) 5, p. 452.

13. See W. Scheler 'Neues Denken über Krieg und Frieden' in *Dt. Ztschr. f. Phil.* 35 (1987) 1, p. 12–20.

14. M. S. Gorbatschow *Polit. Bericht des ZK der KPdSU an den XXVII. Parteitag der KPdSU* (Moscow 1986 German) p. 108.

15. *Friedliche Koexistenz und Sicherheitspartnerschaft. Ein Seminar von Gesellschaftswissenschaftlern der SED und Mitgliedern der Grundwertekommission beim Parteivorstand der SPD*, 27.2.–1.3.1986 in Freudenstadt (proceedings) *IPW-Berichte* 15 (1986) 6, p. 37ff.

16. Cf. *Der Palme—Bericht* Bericht der Unabhängigen Kommission für Abrüstung und Sicherheit (Berlin-West 1982)—*Common Security* (London 1982).

17. Useful in this regard is Militärakademie 'Friederich Engels' (ed.) *Die Philosophie des Friedens im Kampf gegen die Ideologie des Krieges* (Berlin[2] 1986).

18. *Ibid.* Chapter 2 'Das Wesen des Krieges im Zeitalter nuklearer Waffen' here especially p. 83ff.

19. See W. Scheler (note 13), p. 19.

20. M. S. Gorbatschow 'Für eine Welt ohne Kernwaffen, für das Überleben der Menschheit'. Rede vor den Teilnehmern des internationalen Friedensforums in Moskau 16.2.1987 (Berlin 1987) p. 11.

Anne E. Carr

Peace Through a Peaceless Church?

THE SECOND Vatican Council used a vivid expression in one of the phrases it used to describe the Church: 'sacrament of salvation for the world'. The Church, the Council taught, was a sign for the whole world of both intimate union with God and the unity of all humankind. The opening chapter of *Lumen Gentium* noted the 'special urgency' of the Church's task as a sacrament or sign of salvation given the particular conditions of the age in which human social, technical, and cultural interdependence had become so apparent. That was more than twenty years ago.

Today the urgency of the Church's mission is intensified in the conditions of our age—an age that lives in the midst of unceasing global conflict, increasing militarism, deepening ecological crisis, and universal dread of nuclearism and all its terrors. What sign of peace, what new impulse of hope can the Church offer out of its belief in the message of peace that was Jesus' ministry, lived out in his suffering and death at the hands of religious and political authorities? What sign can the Church offer from its belief in Jesus' resurrection by God?[1] What sign can the Church offer to a fragmented world out of its own urgent mission in the continuing life of the Spirit? Or is that mission of peace made incredible because there is no peace within the Church, and because of its long tradition that 'justifies' war?

The Council used many images in defining the Church. But surely the phrase that caught the public imagination was its most inclusive self-description, the biblical understanding of the Church as 'the people of God'. All people in all their difference and diversity—whether Soviets or Buddhists, Muslims or women, black or yellow or red or white—are nevertheless *one people*, God's own people. The Church, in some mysterious way, encompasses all people. And all people are urgently called to peace today. While it is

101

important that leaders in the churches make a special effort to speak for all people, offering a vision and concrete programmes that will effectively unite everyone in the world-wide movement for justice and peace, it is also clear that peacemaking is the responsibility of all.

As people become more informed and concerned about issues of peace, they become more peaceful people in their individual lives and more united with others who share their social concerns. And as these social—indeed global— concerns unite people of all faiths, one senses a movement of the Spirit in unsuspected places, at the edges of the official bureaucracies and hierarchies, in the Church that is the people of God. Ecumenism takes on new meaning in the context of the escalating fear and genuine hope that is the impetus of the world movements for peace. Indeed there is new impetus for unity, justice, and peace—among the churches that claim union in Christ but also in the wider *oecumene*, among the religions of the world, suggesting the need for the articulation of what has been called a 'world political theology'. Such a theology would encompass the burning issues of racism, sexism, classism, world economic justice, clericalism, militarism, and responsibility for the creation in the conviction that there can be no peace without justice among all peoples—and with nature itself. Such a theology would unite all people in the active search for the biblical justice that is fidelity in relationship, for the peace that is of God.

One of the scripture scholars who worked on the peace pastoral of the United States Bishops, *The Challenge of Peace*, describes her personal search for a biblical and feminist alternative to the abstract rationality, relationless logic, and patriarchal power that coloured many of the discussions of the Bishops' Committee with military and political representatives.[2] She found that alternative in recent interpretations of Jesus' parables, and in the extended idea proposed by some biblical scholars that Jesus' whole life is the parable of God's relationship to people and to the world. She also found that alternative in feminist theology's conceptions of *power as enablement* of the oppressed and the marginalised. The biblical interpretations show how Jesus' parables shock and shatter everyday conceptions of logic and technical rationality in their depictions of God's way with humankind: they propose a new logic of God's reign. This logic emphasises the politics of persons and relationships rather than the politics of abstraction, violence, and war. Feminist conceptions of power suggest that 'power to' rather than 'power over' is more consonant with the Christian message of love and justice, reciprocity and mutuality, unity and peace. Together they offer a Christian vision for today that relates the living reality of the Bible to the most urgent and demanding of the signs of the times in the quest for global unity and equality, justice and peace.

This vision entails a new understanding of 'difference'. It is not so much that of French 'deconstructionism'—although study of the intricacies of that school, especially in its feminist developments, can be helpful. Rather it is, simply an understanding of justice, unity and peace that attempts to encompass the difference of the other in its bonds of acceptance in such a way that genuine unity-in-diversity can be struggled toward and achieved. This new understanding and acceptance of difference is a model of unity, justice, and ultimately of peace that does not exclude discussion and debate when conflict and contradiction occur but does insist on the negotiation of real differences in political and legislative, not military or violent ways. It is the non-violence of real willingness—in fact insistence—that the other be accepted in all her or his real diversity. It is non-violent in its suggestion that violence itself is fundamentally rooted in a refusal to accept the other in difference and diversity from oneself, whether that difference be a matter of one's Catholicism, one's Christianity, one's religion, one's sex, one's nation, one's ideology, one's race, one's colour, or one's class.

This conception of acceptance of difference is intrinisically related to feminist theological and ethical analyses of power.[3] This view of power, which has been explicitly part of theological discussion since the appropriation of Whitehead's thought by process theologians, holds that there are two kinds of power. One kind is coercive; it controls, imposes conformity, manipulates, and is basically violent in its demand for its own way. This is the kind of power that characterises military, political, and religious regimes that will not tolerate any difference with, or deviation from, their official positions. Such power is hierarchical and patriarchal, extended 'from the top down', and insists on authority as entailing order, conformity, and obedience. It is fundamentally violent power.

The other kind of power, which Whitehead described as persuasive and that has been adopted by feminist thought in ethical and theological discussion, is the power that lures the other in its effective enablement and empowerment. It emphasises complexity of pattern, relationship, flexibility, spontaneity, mutuality, and interdependence. It emerges 'from the bottom-up' and finds its authority in patterns of shared governance that exist for the sake of mission and service. Feminist theologians have found that this kind of power more appropriately describes the power of the Spirit that is unleashed into the world by Jesus Christ, and that is the only real power of the churches in their universal mission of peace. It is recalled graphically in the words of the Gospel attributed to Jesus:

You know that among the pagans the rulers lord it over them, and their great men make their authority felt. This is not to happen among you. No;

anyone who wants to be great among you must be your servant, and anyone who wants to be first among you must be your slave, just as the Son of Man came not to be served but to serve, and to give his life as a ransom for many (Matt. 20:24).

This biblical vision of service, together with feminist theological understandings of power, suggest a new perspective on the kind of justice, peace, and unity that is the mission of every Christian and of the churches today. It is a mission that involves service and constant dialogue within the diversity of the churches and of the world, not in order to conquer or convert the other to a single way of thinking or acting but to find and make real the transcendent justice, unity, and peace that only God imparts. This does not mean that Christians can wait for peace to be there. It means rather that each must become an active peacemaker in both the personal and the political realms in the living power of the spirit.

The non-violent approach of feminist thought with its familiar slogan, 'the personal is the political', suggests an important analogy among ecclesial approaches to individual, social, and global issues today.[4] In a theological perspective, personal repentance and conversion to the making of peace with God and with one's neighbours in individual life and in issues related to the private realm are modelled and made credible when they are reflected in the patterns adopted in relation to ecclesial governance and the public realm. Similarly, public issues of system and structure, whether of the churches or of nations, require the patient and honest dialogue, reciprocity, and mutuality that characterise personal relationships. If public realm or institutional issues are intractable and admit of legitimate differences in point of view and strategy, so do more private realm concerns. If private realm concerns require attention to the values of life, persons, relationships, and human empowerment, public and global concerns require similar tact and sensitivity.

Liberation and political theologies in our time have made clear the intimate connections between the private concerns of political systems, structures, and institutions. These theologies have demonstrated the eminently practical character of faith in its dual search for God and for human justice, equality, unity and peace in their stress on *praxis* as an authentic source of theory and truth. Such theological understandings, 'timely and even necessary' as they have been described by Roman authorities, suggest the importance of the jointly 'mystical and political' requirements of contemporary Christian faith. A mystical faith knows God by searching personal experience as well as through the texts and teaching of others. A political faith exercises its belief by taking social and public responsibility for the 'incarnation', enfleshment or enactment of the Christian vision into the framework of institutions, systems, structures—on ecclesial, national, and international levels. A mystical-political faith attempts to unite body and soul, spirit and flesh, the individual and the social, the public and the private, beyond the world-denying spirtualities of some past interpretations of Christianity.[5]

In this context nuclear terror has been aptly described as the 'dark night' of our world, a situation of dread, impasse, and helplessness that confounds individuals and churches, nations and blocs. And, it has been affirmed, the God of peace is to be found in the call to repentance, conversion, and peace-making that will mobilise Christians and the Church itself to search for and to find the ways of peace which the biblical *shalom* suggests.[6]

The urgency today of the world-wide call for peace has already united many Christians and is beginning to unite the still-divided Christian churches in a way that goes beyond official ecumenical discussions of historic differences in ritual and belief. Important as these discussions are, the urgency of the call for peace today impels all to beg the leadership and the members of all the Christian churches for those concrete signs of peacemaking which will give effective witness to the message of Jesus and the power of the Holy Spirit in the world today. As the self-named sacrament of the world's salvation, the Catholic Church is especially begged to intensify the efforts begun in Assisi in October of 1986 when the Pope gathered the leaders of all religions of the world to pray for peace. For there is an interdependence among the finding of peace in the world, peace in the Roman Catholic church and among the Christian churches. The universality of Christianity, which is so disputed in the variety and irreducibility of the world's religions, at least means the extension of Jesus' message of peace and the gentle power of the Holy Spirit to its own members and to the whole world in its dark night.

Notes

1. See Carol Frances Jegen, BVM *Jesus the Peacemaker* (Kansas City 1986) for an extended study of Jesus' message, and his death and resurrection, as the Christian model of peacemaking.
2. Juliana Casey *Where is God Now? Nuclear Terror Feminism and the Search for God* (Kansas City 1987).
3. See, e.g. Beverly Wildung Harrison *Making the Connections: Essays in feminist Social Ethics* ed. Carol S. Robb (Boston: Beacon Press 1985) and *Women's Consciousness, Women's Conscience* ed. Barbara Hilkert Andolsen, Christine E. Gudorf, and Mary D. Pellauer (New York 1985).
4. For a discussion of the several meanings of non-violence see Kenneth R. Himes 'Pacifism in the Catholic Church', *The Ecumenist* 25:3 (March–April, 1987) pp. 44–48.
5. Rosemary Radford Ruether *Sexism and God-Talk: Toward A Feminist Theology* (Boston 1983).
6. Casey *Where is God Now?* pp. 150–152.

PART IV

Synthesis

Jürgen Moltmann

Peace the Fruit of Justice

1. THE CHURCH: PRODUCT AND INSTRUMENT OF DIVINE PEACE[1]

DOES POLITICAL peace have a theological dimension? And religious peace a political dimension?

Many churches are still uncertain whether the Church ought to take part in debates about 'secular peace', or restrict itself, its preaching and pastoral efforts, to 'peace with God' and the 'spiritual peace' of individuals.[2] If the Church concerns itself with political matters, then, those of another political opinion maintain, it reduces peace with God to a political level and 'shalomises' the peace which is from above. If the Church does not concern itself thus, those who are committed and politically active say, then its silence makes it party to the force which produces unfreedom, for whoever remains silent in the face of evil is an accomplice of evil (Martin Luther King). To avoid such unprofitable contention, I shall begin with the event which makes the Church *Church*, and which decides each person's Christian existence: the justifying and peacegiving action of God in Jesus Christ. Paul sums up the Christian message of divine justice thus: 'Jesus our Lord ... was put to death for our trespasses and raised for our justification' (Rom. 4:25). In Colossians the same news is presented as a reconciling message of divine peace: 'For in him [Jesus Christ] all the fulness of God was pleased to dwell, and through him to reconcile to himself all things, whether on earth or in heaven, making peace by the blood of his cross' (1:19–20). Everything which is the Church, and similarly everything which ordains Christian existence, is indebted to this justifying, reconciling and peace-giving divine action through Jesus Christ. What was done for us on the Cross on Golgotha, and in his resurrection from

109

the dead, was the work of God and precedes everything which the Church does and says. The Church is the fruit of God's expiatory suffering and is the creation of God's justifying action. In both together it is the work of God's will to peace. Because God creates justice, Christ is. Because God establishes peace there is a Church. Therefore Jesus Christ's Church has to be a Church of peace. Accordingly all divine service in the Church of Christ begins with a salute of peace, and the Church's blessing is pronounced with the peace of God, which passes all understanding.

But every gift gives rise to an appropriate task. The Church of Christ is the work of divine justification and peacegiving, and is also and just as seriously the instrument of that divine action. The justification of the sinner gives rise to the sanctification of the justified, so that they may do the work of justice in the world. The reconciliation of those troubled by lack of peace prompts the mission of the reconciled as peacegivers in this world without peace. No other response from Christians to the justifying word of God would be appropriate to the dynamic spirit of that divine word. Those reconciled to God become immediately and inalienably the peacegivers of their world. To be sure, the creative activity of God and the responsive activity of human beings are not on the same level, for God is God and humans are humans. But we cannot separate the two levels. People owe their peace to the action of God, but God assigns everything to new human activity. God justifies in order to sanctify. God summons in order to send. And God gives peace that there may be peacegivers. Anyone who remains personally content with the peace of God in itself, and does not become a peacegiver, has not experienced the inward thrust of divine peace and does not know the divine Spirit.[3]

As the work and instrument of divine peace, the Church exists in various societies and at various social levels, and therefore in the thick of economic, social and political conflicts. These conflicts extend deep into the Church itself. Every Christian experiences them, is affected by them, and accordingly has to inquire into his or her own peace-giving potential in his or her own particular context. Political theology refines awareness of the political context in which churches and Christians actually exist. Of course some may behave as if that had nothing to do with the Church or the believing spirit of Christians, but such conscious repression helps no one. The more effectively a church acknowledges its social, political and cultural environment, the more faithfully it can carry out its divine commission, and the more effective an instrument of divine peace it can become. The declarations of the Latin American Catholic bishops' conferences at Medellin in 1968 and at Puebla in 1978 are exemplary in this respect. The fact that we in the 'First World' do not achieve anything of the same order demonstrates, I think, the new 'Babylonian captivity' of the Church, which is only non-Babylonian in that the Church does not experience it as captivity on account of the privileges which it enjoys in western society. But a Church which accepts such privileges and accordingly says nothing about the injustice perpetrated by society, is not a Church which acknowledges Christ alone and only Christ as its Lord. The task of political theology is not some kind of 'politicisation of the Church', but the necessary christianisation of existence and of the functions of the Church in modern societies.

The major overall conflicts of the world today are reflected in life's many small conflicts. They may be summed up in the paradox that we live in one world which is nevertheless divided.

 1. The development of the scientifico-technological civilisation of modern times has produced the noisome injustice of the 'Third World'. By that I mean both the poor people of the 'Third World' nations and the growing poverty in the 'First World' industrial nations.

2. The same modern civilisation has produced for its supposed security the 'system of nuclear deterrence', which enables the terrible end of this world to become a reality at any time. The system of deterrence threatens an opponent with universal destruction and therefore represents the hitherto most inclusive form of deadly violence and organised lack of peace.

3. This modern civilisation buys its technological successes by means of a progressive, reckless destruction of nature. Every year many varieties of plants and animals vanish for ever. The atmosphere is irreparably destroyed. Forests are defoliated. Deserts spread. The so-called ecological crisis of modern industrial societies is only a euphemism for the ecological death of nature and the ecological suicide of the human race. An atomic war is apocalypse now; the destruction of nature is an amortised apocalypse. The Chernobyl disaster of 1986 was a warning of both developments. The overall situation in which the Church, which has intimately experienced the experience of divine peace, is summoned to establish peace was tellingly characterised by Mikhail Gorbachov when he said: 'The human race has lost its immortality'. The human race as such is under deathly threat from human beings. It could die out.

The major churches today agree: 1. War can no longer be a political option; 2. the spirit of the logic and practice of the nuclear deterrence system has to be rejected; and 3. a just peace can be the only legitimate goal of politics.

2. HOPE AND PRACTICE OF PEACE

The great saving word in the Old Testament is *shalom*. Because it is so inclusive it is difficult to define. It means the blessed joy of a successful life. It means the sanctification of life in (the reality) of all its relations. It means a just life of which it may be said: 'See, it is very good and no more is needed. It is the fulness of life in the presence of the living God. It is the fulness of life in the mutual love of human beings. It is the fulness of life in the community of creation with all other creatures. Characteristically, *shalom* is neither divided nor limited. Here it is impossible to distinguish salvation from well-being, the peace of God and secular peace, the soul and politics. *Shalom* tends to universality.[4]

That is why, even in the Old Testament, *shalom* became the prophetic word of promise of the future divine salvation for the entire creation. As long as violence and unjust suffering are features of the earth, there is no *shalom*. As long as death reigns, God's *shalom* is still a long way off. Whatever of shalom Israel experienced historically as a nation, and whatever the individual believer experiences of *shalom*, is merely, therefore, a premonition and an indication of the universal *shalom* to come. In every individual fulfilment of the divine promise of *shalom*, there is the experience of the still unfulfilled promise of *shalom* for everyone. Therefore every historical taste of *shalom* awakens longing for the future of *shalom* fulfilled. Israel found *shalom* in its covenant with God. But this covenant made Israel a 'light for the nations'. In regard to Israel God is interested not so much in Israel as such but in universal righteousness and the peace of nations. Israel is nothing more than the promise made flesh of *shalom* for the nations and for the whole of creation. The messianic promises of the prophet Isaiah show this clearly. The Messiah and his people bring 'everlasting peace' (Isa. 9:6) into the world, because they 'bring justice' (Isa. 11:4) for the poor and wretched.

Christians recognised this promised Messiah in Jesus, because through him and in his community they experienced the salvation, the *shalom*, of God. In Jesus' proclamation of the kingdom of God to the poor, justice is accorded to those who suffer injustice. In Jesus' proclamation of the kingdom of God the sick receive health and the dying life. In his proclamation, outcasts and aliens are accorded community. Through his surrender to death on the cross and in his resurrection from the dead eternal life is made apparent: a life in the full *shalom* of God, because it has vanquished death. Christians live from the fulfilment of the divine promise of *shalom* through Jesus and in Jesus. But because this promise is fulfilled only in him, but not visibly in the world, *shalom* already exists in faith but also simultaneously in the future in hope. Christ is the unique commencement of the universal *shalom* of God in this world and in our history.

In communion with Jesus the Messiah, human beings experience the presence of God's *shalom* in the Spirit. That is, the experiences of turning from death to life, of rebirth into hope, of the recreation of love, and of revolt against violence and indifference. In the experience of the creative Spirit what was thought to be impossible becomes possible, the weak are made strong, those deprived of justice receive it, the rejected are loved, and peace becomes possible.

Experiences of the prophetic and messianic anticipations of the universal *shalom* of God in Israel and in the Church afford the following prospects for the action of peace:

1. Peace is not a condition but a process, not a possession but a way.

2. Peace is not the absence of power, but the presence of justice. In peace research we distinguish now between a negative and a positive concept of peace.

The negative definition maintains that peace is non-war: that is, absence of the open and of the collective use of force. To define the negative notion of peace more specifically, peace is the absence of force, of need, of unfreedom and of fear. This negative understanding of peace obtains when statesmen opine that in the last twenty years nuclear deterrent systems have 'preserved the peace'. Of course this claim is quite untenable, and moreover peace is here confused with armistice. And nothing is said about the cost of the deterrent. The greater the cost of ensuring that there is peace, however, the less justification there is for calling what is thereby assured, peace. Though it is very easy to agree on a negative definition of peace, it is quite unsatisfactory.[5]

The positive definition, however, defines peace as a state of social justice, democratic conflict-solving and international cooperation. Many people think this is utopian, but the negative notion of peace does not work without positive elements.

The Christian concept of peace unites both definitions: peace is the absence of force, suffering and injustice, and the presence of justice, freedom and a life in communion with God, other people and nature. The service of peace then means resistance to force and war, and is a service to justice and to life.

Peace researchers differentiate between peace as a state and peace as a process.

Anyone defining peace as a state must either reduce expectations of peace to such an extent that they fit an historical condition, or wait here for peace in history, but in vain. While people continue to enrich themselves at others' expense, while people continue to oppress others, and while people continue to be afraid of others, there is no peace. Peace as a state is a utopia, and the worst utopia of this kind is that of the status quo. Only those who have a good life-style think they live in peace. They ignore those who have to live impoverished lives.

Therefore it is better to see peace as an historical process, with instances of progress, and with setbacks. On the road to peace we have to reduce violence, armaments, and structural force, and we have to build community and reciprocal trust. On the road to peace, we are concerned with the diminution of economic exploitation and to establish a just universal economic system. On the road to peace we are interested in removing unfreedom and in ensuring the democratic participation of the people in political decisions.

In the Christian interpretation, historical peace is a multiple process of anticipation of that universal peace which the coming kingdom of God will fulfil. Here and now, already, Christians live by virtue of the peace of the kingdom which is to come, and wherever possible introduce that peace into this violent world. Christians are not oriented to 'the beyond', as some would say, but introduce the beyond into the here-and-now. When it is lived authentically, Christian faith is not the 'opium of the people' but the power which enables the people to be liberated.

3. PEACE THE FRUIT OF JUSTICE

The other great saving word in the Old Testament is *zedaka*, justice. 'In the Old Testament there is no concept which is so very important for all human relations as that of *zedaka*.'[6] It is the yardstick not only for the relationship between people and God, but for their relations with one another and for their relations with the rest of creation. *Zedaka* does not mean—as in the Graeco-Roman world from which we derive out notions of justice, *justitia*, behaviour appropriate to a predetermined absolute ethical standard—but living loyalty to community. The God of the Exodus and of the Sinaitic covenant is the faithful God. His truth is that he remains loyal to his promise and thereby makes it trustworthy and reliable. Accordingly, Psalm 143:1 prays; 'In thy faithfulness answer me, in thy righteousness'. By his covenant God enters into a community together with the nation of his choice. his righteousness is that he maintains this covenant. The righteousness of the people is that for its part it maintains the covenant and its law. If the nation becomes disloyal and godless, then God's loyalty to his covenant becomes apparent as grace, which makes the unrighteous righteous by recalling them to the covennant. Hence Psalm 32:1 says: 'Behold, a king will reign in righteousness'. The great feast of reconciliation is the major feast in Israel. It celebrates divine justice as reconciling grace. 'The notion of a punitive *zedaka* has no support—it would be a *contradictio in adjecto*' (G. von Rad, op cit. p. 375). God's justice is always saving, always brings justice and always establishes righteousness. In his righteousness God does not merely confirm what is just and what is unjust, but proffers justice to those without it and shows the doers of violence the injustice of their ways. Through his justice God creates peace, substantial peace.

There is no peace in oppression. Where injustice and violence rule there is no peace, even though everything is quiet and no one dare protest. Those are false prophets who then cry 'Peace, peace!', when what actually prevails is not peace but only death. It is not the Church of Christ but the religion of the anti-Christ which preaches 'reconciliation' for the sake of such a peace in any society in which justice is trampled down, as the 'Kairos Document' of critical and prophetic Christians in South Africa rightly says.[7] In the Old and New Testaments, it is theologically clear that justice has precedence over peace, because justice creates peace, but peace does not bring about justice. Therefore the peace activity of the Church and of Christians has to be directed to justice. Whoever brings justice to the wretched serves peace, even if he or she is delivered up to the anger of the rich. Whoever takes up the cause of the despised serves peace, even if he or she delivers himself or herself up to the hatred of the self-righteous. The WCC Conference in Vancouver in 1983 correctly placed the convenant for justice in first place before the convenant for peace and for the life of creation.

I should like to relate the biblical tradition of divine *zedaka*, and the *zedaka* of human beings and creation to our notions of justice, in order then to direct righteous activity to the establishment of *shalom* in our world.

An earlier idea of European legal culture defined justice as '*justitia distributiva*'. '*Suum cuique*' is the watchword: to each his or her own. This nimble formula unites legal equality ('to each ...') with the actual difference of people ('his or her own'). Not the same to each, but to each according to his or her means. This idea of justice is however largely related to property and work. Every human being has the right to life, food and freedom, as is appropriate to specifically human nature.

The individually and communually relevant idea of justice extends beyond this materially directed concept. It consists in the acknowledgment of the other in his or her otherness, and in acceptance of the other in his or her specificity for supplementation of one's own self. Reciprocal acknowledgment and acceptance produce a just community. This undoubtedly corresponds to the Christian idea of justice as justification: 'Welcome one another, therefore, as Christ has welcomed you, for the glory of God' (Rom. 15:7). This individually related notion of justice is also the concept of justice at the basis of modern societal ideas of covenant and contract.

Finally, justice may not be formulated ideally. Instead, we have to inquire into actual justice in a world of violence and injustice. In such situations justice pre-eminently assumes the form of siding with the powerless and with victims of violence. This partisan acknowledgment is to be found unmistakably throughout the Old and New Testaments. 'The Lord lifts up those who are bowed down; the Lord loves the righteous ... the Lord lifts up the downtrodden, he casts the wicked to the ground' (Ps. 146/147). Just as unequivocally it gives rise to the commission: Execute 'justice for the fatherless and the widow' (Deut. 10:18). That is the divine law of mercy, the sympathetic option for the poor, which Jesus so emphatically showed us. 'Mercy' does not mean being soft-hearted, as it were, but that those deprived of justice receive what is due to them. The weak have a right to the protection of mercy, and the strong are duty-bound to be merciful. 'Mercy' is not mere gentle benevolence, but feeling commitment to the rights of the other. Therefore it is not something outside the order of justice but itself productive of justice. Like the acknowledgment of the other, the exercise of mercy towards the weak is the basis of all orders of justice which serve the cause of peace. 'Peace is the fruit of justice ...'—I should like to illustrate this principle in terms of two choices: that of love of one's enemy and that of the non-violent suppression of force.

Anyone who gets into an argument and takes part in conflict is subject to the law of retribution: an eye for an eye, a tooth for a tooth. Whoever relates to the enemy in accordance with this law, is in a dilemma from which there is no exit. He or she must become the enemy's enemy, hating the hater, moulded by the enemy. If evil is met with evil, then one evil always follows on the other, and is justified by the other evil. That is fatal. Liberation is possible only if there is no thinking of enemy as enemy. The love which Jesus puts in the place of retribution is love of one's enemies (Matt. 5:43ff.).

Love of an enemy is not retributory, but accommodating and creative love. Whoever repays evil with good does not merely react but creates something new, no longer allowing the enemy to prescribe the rules of the game. Love of one's enemy demands a great deal of sovereignty. The more liberated from fear one is, the greater the success of love of one's enemy. Love of an enemy, however, can never mean subjection to the enemy, but must intend the intelligent and creative suppression of enmity. It is a kind of love which seeks to subvert enmity (P. Lapide). Love of an enemy does not ask, How can I protect myself from this enemy? but, How can I free the enemy from his inimical attitude? Love of one'e enemy makes the enemy conscious of his or her own responsibility. Therefore love of one's enemy cannot be condemned as mere piety but as a true ethic of responsibility. Love of one's enemy applies not only in private life where it is especially problematical, but in political life, where we do not ensure that we have peace by exterminating all our enemies, but only by ensuring that we overcome enmities and assume responsibility for our common security. The politics of love of one's enemy demands thinking along with and for the others. The question is not how western Europe can protect itself from the 'Russian threat', but how we can construct a common order for peace in Europe between West and East. That presumes the demilitarisation and democratisation of our thinking.[8]

Love of one's enemy gives rise to non-violent suppression of force. That sounds paradoxical, but is not so. Non-violence does not mean depoliticisation, for a distinction has to be made between 'force' and 'power'.[9] 'Power' is the justified, legitimate and legal use of force. In this sense the modern state possesses the so-called 'monopoly of force' in our society. By 'force' I understand the unjust and unjustifiable use of power. We speak thus of 'naked force' or 'brutality'. In our societies Christianity has been unable to get rid of barbaric violence. But it has made it necessary to justify every use of force, especially a state's use of force. Justice also restricts the use of force by a state, not only internally in respect of citizens of the state in question, but externally in regard to other states and to humankind as a whole. Threatening the human race with a nuclear holocaust is an act of force which cannot be justified in any way. The first form of suppression of force is the association of all exercise of power with justice. There follows the duty to resist all unjust uses of power, whether illegal or illegitimate or directed against human rights. Non-violence does not exclude a power struggle, if that struggle is concerned to keep power in line with justice. Anyone who resists actively or passively under a public rule of violence is only doing his or her duty as a citizen, and supporting the restoration of justice or the obtaining of justice for all. That person is justified in using all instruments of power, but may not use brutality, because that would compromise his or her own goals. Hence the promotion of disarmament until all nations are incapable of attacking one another.

The power of nations which suffer from the rule of violence is not terror but solidarity. General solidarity deprives violent rulers of all appearance of justice and takes the fright out of their threats. In our own times we have a number of instances of peoples overcoming military dictatorships in non-violent ways: Greece, Argentina, the Philippines. The rule of violence is weakly grounded when it is isolated and deprived both of trust and of fear. The non-violent suppression of force is certainly possible. Of course, it can demand martyrdom. We think of Gandhi and of Martin Luther King. We think above all of Jesus himself. When we think of him, then we also discover that not only active behaviour has liberating power and leads to 'success', but that suffering too has a liberating because reconciling power and can become a 'blessing' to many. 'The blood of the martyrs is the seed of the Church' was how it went in the ancient Roman empire. That is true in a somewhat different sense of the seed of peace in justice, which a number of small groups sow today.

How can Christians, communities and the churches organise their commitment to peace through justice?

I assume that peace is the flesh of justice and that for that reason justice is the soul of peace. If that is the case, then the Church must be seen as the body of divine peace, and testify to peace through its own existence, not merely through pastoral letters and political demonstrations.

The Church exists in various social forms. Here I list in descending order: 1. the universal Church, 2. the national Church, 3. the local parish, 4. the voluntary group and movement. The service of peace must take various forms on these different levels. I think it is reasonable to make distinctions here, so that there is no mutual overloading.

I shall begin down below with the voluntary group:

1. Commitment to peace always demands a personal commitment to non-violent action, and personal readiness for sacrifice. Hence peace groups everywhere and the 'Third-World groups' for social justice. In such cases concerned people come together voluntarily and work at an actual task which they acknowledge and undertake in common as their own task. They develop their own readiness to participate in demonstrations and in social action. Together with this readiness for public action, a special form of spirituality comes into being: Dietrich Bonhoeffer called this new way of life 'resistance and submission'. Taizé calls it 'contemplation and struggle'. 'Mysticism and liberation' is the watchword of the basic communities in Latin America. These peace groups come together regionally and internationally through 'networks', and in this way construct a form of ecumenism from below. But these are groups and movements and networks of like-minded people. And so the Catholic peace movement Pax Christi has difficulties with the German Catholic hierarchy. And the basic communities in Latin America are not to the liking of all bishops. And the Christian peace movement in the Reformed Church in Germany is looked on with considerable misgiving. The reason is not only that the representatives of institutions fear the uncontrollable spontaneity of these groups and movements, but that the local parishes consist not of like-minded but of differently-minded people. The 'Union of Catholic Soldiers' in Germany polemicises against Pax Christi, and the Protestant forces' chaplains attack the Reformed peace movement in our Church. What then is to be expected from the local parish? And what required?

2. The local parish is the product of the proclamation of the gospel and of baptism. It usually assembles on Sunday morning for divine service. People assemble who think differently about peace and justice. They do not come together in order to meet politically like-minded people in the same church. Therefore the local church parish can hardly become a peace group. I think

that its witness to peace is to be found on another level. Hitherto the local parish was largely a religious community and a community for divine service in the ritual sense. If however it has regard to the whole gospel of Christ, it will be transformed into a living community. The more closely Christians in the local parish live together, the more aware they beocme of the social, economic and political conflicts in which they exist, and inquire into justice and peace in these conflicts. The more they recognise that divine salvation intends the entire restoration or sanctification of creaturely health, the more aware they will become of their own duties for the healing of the social and political sicknesses of the society in which they live. In addition to divine service, the parish assembly then becomes important too, for the working groups report to it and local tasks are discussed there. It is also the place where the peace groups can contribute their experiences to the local parish, so that local parishes can get going with the learning process of peace.

3. The local or national churches are neither local communities or parishes nor peace movements. Theirs is a regional context—that of the area covered by the church. They have to face the conflicts which prevail in such areas, and in regional peace conferences try to replace mutual assured destruction with mutual trust. That is the 'European churches' conference' for a divided Europe. Its political counterpart is the KSZE conferences: conferences for the construction of 'trust-conducive measures' and reciprocal security partnerships between West- and East-European nations.

Finally, the universal Church to date has been visible only on a denominational level: in Rome, in Geneva, and in the international organisations of the various denominations. It will be perceptible only when that all-Christian 'convocation for peace' is in preparation at which Christianity as a whole testifies before a mortally threatened human universe with the justice of God, the peace of nations and the life of creation.

4. The watchword for all organisational forms of the Church is 'Think globally—act locally!' To make that possible, communication in the churches has to be improved. The pastoral letters, encyclicals, handouts and memoranda on peace which we have met with to date have for the most part descended by one-way channels. They have seldom reached the basis and are scarcely taken seriously. Moreover the reports on the experiences of the basis are hardly ever read and considered 'up above'. It would seem to be the duty of church leaders to receive the experiences and questions from below, and to transmit them further. Only when the churches at all levels, in national and local churches, local parishes and communities and peace groups, start a common learning process for justice and peace, can they really begin to speak with the one voice which will enable them to be heard.

Translated by J. G. Cumming

Notes

1. In this article I consciously adopt some ideas and formulations from the paper given by Dr H. Falcke of Erfurt GDR, on 'Theology of Peace in the one, divided World' at the session of the *Gesellschaft für Evangelische Theologie* in February 1987, to show that Christians in East and West can speak with one voice on this matter. Falcke's paper is to be published by Christian Kaiser Verlag of Munich in spring 1988, in a symposium on 'Peace Theology—Liberation Theology'.

2. Cf. in this respect the symposia *Aktion Sühnezeichewn-Friedensdienste* (Eds.), *Christen im Streit um den Frieden* (Freiburg 1982); German Bishops' Conference (Eds.) *Hirtenworte zu Krieg und Frieden* (Cologne 1983).

3. As against the 'Armaggedon theology' of such cynical apocalypticists as Hal Lindsay *The Late Great Planet Earth* (Grand Rapids 1970), *id.*, *The 1980s: Countdown to Armaggedon, King of Prussia* (Pa. 1980).

4. N. Lohfink *Unsere grossen Wörter. Das alte Testament zu Themen dieser Jahre* (Freiburg 1977).

5. E. Eppler *Die tödliche Utopie der Sicherheit* (Hamburg 1983).

6. G. von Rad *Theologie des Alten Testaments*, I (Munich 2nd ed. 1957) p. 368.

7. *Challenge to the Church. A Theological Comment on the Political Crisis in South Africa. The 'Kairos Document'* (Braamfontein 1985).

8. This requirement was also put before the participants in the international forum 'For a world without nuclear weapons, for the survival of Humankind', Moscow, February 1987, by General Secretary Gorbachev: *Für die Unsterblichkeit der menschlichen Zivilisation* (Beienrode 1987).

9. See in greater detail, J. Moltmann *Politische Theologie—Politische Ethik* (Munich-Mainz 1984) pp. 124ff.

Contributors

ANNE CARR, BVM was born in Chicago. She studied at Marquette University, Milwaukee and at the University of Chicago Divinity School. She taught at Mundelein College, Chicago and Indiana University before returning to the University of Chicago where she is now in the Theology faculty. She is the author of *The Theological Method of Karl Rahner* (1977); *A Search for Wisdom and Spirit: Thomas Merton's Theology of the Self* (1987); and *A Transforming Grace: Tradition, Symbol, and the Experience of Women* (1988). She has published many articles in such journals as *Theological Studies, Horizons, Theology Today*, and *Chicago Studies*.

G. CLARKE CHAPMAN, Jr. is Professor of Religion, Moravian College, Bethlehem, Pennsylvania. An ordained elder in the United Methodist Church, he studied at Boston University where he obtained his PhD in systematic theology in 1963. He also studied at Eberhard-Karls University, Tübingen, in 1962 and in 1972. He helped to found and is chairperson of the Interfaith Peace Resource Center at Bethlehem. His published writings include *Facing the Nuclear Heresy: A Call to Reformation* (1986): '*Black Power' Schwarze Gewalt, Schwarze Theologie*; 'Amerikanische Theologie im Schatten der Bombe', *Evangelische Theologie* 47:1 (Jan./Feb. 1987) (and forthcoming in English translation, *Union Seminary Quarterly Review* June 1987); 'Hope and the Ethics of Formation: Moltmann as an Interpreter of Bonhoeffer' *Studies in Religion/Sciences Religieuses* 12:4 (1983); 'Bonhoeffer: Resource for Liberation Theology', *Union Seminary Quarterly Review* 36:4 (Summer 1981).

HANS DIEFENBACHER was born 1954 and studied political economy at Freiburg, Heidelberg and Cassel universities. He obtained his doctorate in politics and was appointed Research fellow in economics at the Protestant Institute for Interdisciplinary Research, Heidelberg. Recent publications include: with Hans G. Nutzinger (Ed.) *Mitbestimmung in Betrieb und Verwaltung* (Heidelberg 1986); 'Natur und ökonomische Theorie', *Universitas* 11, 1986; 'Was ist(uns) die Natur wert', in H. Timm (Ed.); *Wie grün darf die Zukunft sein?* (Gütersloh 1987); with J. Johnson, 'Energy Forecasting in West Germany: Confrontation and Convergence' T. Baumgartner and A. Midttun (Eds.) *The Politics of Energy Forecasting* (Oxford 1987).

IGNACIO ELLACURÍA was born in the Basque Country in 1930, and has lived in Latin America since 1949. He studied theology under Karl Rahner at Innsbruck from 1958–62, and gained a doctorate in philosophy with a thesis on the thought of Zubiri. He is now Director of the Centre for Theological Studies in El Salvador. His latest book is *Freedom made Flesh* (1976), and he contributes regularly to reviews in El Salvador and other countries.

JOACHIM GARSTECKI was born in Magdeburg in 1942. He studied Theology in the Philosophical-Theological Faculty in Erfurt. Thereafter he worked with the Catholic Pastoral Office in Magdeburg from 1965 to 1970. Since 1974, he has been involved as an expert on peace discussions in the Theology student section of the Association of Protestant Churches of the GDR, in Berlin. He was co-editor of *Menschenrechte in christlicher Verantwortung* (1978) and has contributed essays on peace in ethical and political terms to various journals.

STANLEY HAUERWAS is Professor of Theological Ethics in the Divinity School at Duke University. He also serves as Director of Graduate Studies in Religion at Duke. His publications include *The Peaceable Kingdom: A Primer in Christian Ethics* (1983) and *Against the Nations: War and Survival in a Liberal Society* (1985).

WOLFGANG HUBER was born in 1942, and is Professor of systematic theology and ethics in the theological faculty of Heidelberg University. He is a member of the research unit of the Protestant academic community in Heidelberg. Recent publications include *The Struggle for Truth and the Ability for Peace* (1980); *Living on God's Earth. Biblical Insights* (1985); with D. Ritschl and T. Sundermeier: *Ecumenical Existence Today* (1986); *Protestantism and Protest* (1987).

ENDA McDONAGH is a priest of the Archdiocese of Tuam, and Professor of Moral Theology at Maynooth. Recent publications include: *Irish Challenges to Theology* Ed. (1987) *Between Chaos and New Creation* (1987).

JÜRGEN MOLTMANN was born in Hamburg in 1926 and is a member of the German Reformed Church. He studied at the University of Göttingen, where he took further degrees and became a qualified university teacher of theology. From 1958 to 1963 he was professor at the Kirchliche Hochschule at Wuppertal and from 1963 to 1967 professor of systematic theology at Bonn University. He is now professor of systematic theology at Tübingen University. He is chairman of the 'Gesellschaft für Evangelische Theologie'.

His publications include: *Prädestination und Perseveranz* (1961), *Theology of Hope* (Eng. tr. 1967), *Perspektiven der Theologie* (1968), *Der Mensch* (4th ed. 1979), *Die ersten Freigelassenen der Schöpfung* (5th ed. 1976), *The Crucified God* (Eng. tr. 1975), *Kirche in der Kraft des Geistes* (1975), *Zukunft der Schöpfung* (1977), *Trinität und Reich Gottes* (1980).

DIETMAR MIETH was born in 1940 and has been Professor of Theological Ethics in Tübingen since 1981. His publications include: *Epik und Ethik Gotteserfahrung—Weltverantwortung* (1982); *Die neuen Tugenden* (1984); *Arbeit und Menschenwürde* (1985).

DAMASKINOS PAPANDREOU, born in Greece in 1936, gained his diploma in theology from the Theological Institute at Halki, Turkey, in 1959, and from then until 1965 continued his studies in Church history, comparative religion and in the philosophy of religion at Bonn and Marburg, gaining his doctorate in theology at the University of Athens in 1966. From 1965 until 1969 he was prior of the Orthodox monastic centre at Taizé, and since 1969 he has been director of the Orthodox Centre of the Ecumenical Patriarchate at Chambésy, Geneva, and secretary for the preparatory work for the Holy and Great Council of the Orthodox Church. In 1970 he was ordained to the episcopate and elected Metropolitan of Tranoupolis, and since 1982 he has been Metropolitan of Switzerland and Exarch of Europe. Since 1974 he has been an associate professor at the theological faculty of Lucerne, and since 1986 a member of the executive council of the Council of European Churches.

His publications include: *Die Gründung und Organissation der armenischen Kirche bis sum IV. Ökumenischen Konzil* (dissertation, 1966); (with R. Erni) *Eucharistiegemeinschaft. Der Standpunkt der Orthodoxie* (1974); *Theological Dialogue: An Orthodox Perspective* (Thessalonica, 1986, in Greek). He edited *Stimmen der Orthodoxie. Zu Grundfragen des II. Vatkanums* (1969) and is editor of *Episkepsis* (since 1970), *Synodica* (since 1974), *Etudes théologiques* (since 1980) and is co-editor of *Una Sancta* (since 1974). He has contributed numerous articles on questions of the preparatory work for the forthcoming Holy and Great Council and on ecumenism. A collection of these has been published, edited by W. Schneemelcher: *Orthodoxie und Ökumene. Gesammelte Aufsätze von Damaskinos Papandreou*, Stuttgart 1986.

ROSEMARY RUETHER is the Georgia Harkness Professor of Applied Theology at the Garrett-Evangelical Theological Seminary in Evanston, Illinois, USA. She is the author of numerous books and articles on feminist and liberation theology, among them *Sexism and God-Talk: Toward a Feminist Theology* (Beacon Press 1983) and *Womanguides: Texts for Feminist*

124   CONTRIBUTORS

Theology (Beacon Press 1985). She has completed a manuscript on feminist liturgical communities (*Women-Church: The Theology and Practice of Feminist Liturgical Communities*) to be published by Harper and Row in the summer of 1986.

JON SOBRINO comes from the Basque country and was born on 27 December 1938. He has been a Jesuit since 1956. Since 1957 he has belonged to the Central America Province and usually lives in El Salvador. He was ordained priest in 1969. He graduated in Philosophy and Arts from St Louis University 1963 and MSc in Engineering from St Louis University 1965. His publications include: *The True Church and the Poor* (1984); *Jesus in Latin America* (1986).

LUKAS VISCHER was born in 1926 in Basle and is Professor of Ecumenical Theology at Berne University and Principal of the Evangelical Centre Oekumene Schweiz in Berne. Since 1950 he has been a pastor of the Swiss Evangelical Reformed Church and from 1953–61 pastor at Herblingen near Schaffhausen. In 1961 he became a member of the Faith and Order secretariat of the World Council of Churches in Geneva and from 1965 Director of the secretariat. He was elected in 1982 at the General Assembly of the World Alliance of Reformed Churches in Ottawa as Head of the Theological Department. His publications have been mainly in the fields of church unity, relationship of church to society, ecumenical theology and the ecumenical movement.

CONCILIUM

Polarization in the Church. Ed.
Hans Küng and Walter Kasper.
0 8164 2572 8 156pp.
Spiritual Revivals. Ed. Christian
Duquoc and Casiano Floristán.
0 8164 2573 6 156pp.
Power and the Word of God. Ed.
Franz Bockle and Jacques Marie
Pohier. 0 8164 2574 4 156pp.
The Church as Institution. Ed.
Gregory Baum and Andrew
Greeley. 0 8164 2575 2 168pp.
Politics and Liturgy. Ed. Herman
Schmidt and David Power.
0 8164 2576 0 156pp.
Jesus Christ and Human Freedom.
Ed. Edward Schillebeeckx and
Bas van Iersel. 0 8164 2577 9
168pp.
The Experience of Dying. Ed.
Norbert Greinacher and Alois
Müller. 0 8164 2578 7 156pp.
Theology of Joy. Ed. Johannes
Baptist Metz and Jean-Pierre
Jossua. 0 8164 2579 5 164pp.
The Mystical and Political
Dimension of the Christian Faith.
Ed. Claude Geffré and Gustavo
Guttierez. 0 8164 2580 9 168pp.
The Future of the Religious Life.
Ed. Peter Huizing and William
Bassett. 0 8164 2094 7 96pp.
Christians and Jews. Ed. Hans
Küng and Walter Kasper.
0 8164 2095 5 96pp.
Experience of the Spirit. Ed. Peter
Huizing and William Bassett.
0 8164 2096 3 144pp.
Sexuality in Contemporary
Catholicism. Ed. Franz Bockle
and Jacques Marie Pohier.
0 8164 2097 1 126pp.
Ethnicity. Ed. Andrew Greeley
and Gregory Baum. 0 8164 2145 5
120pp.
Liturgy and Cultural Religious
Traditions. Ed. Herman Schmidt
and David Power. 0 8164 2146 2
120pp.
A Personal God? Ed. Edward
Schillebeeckx and Bas van Iersel.
0 8164 2149 8 142pp.
The Poor and the Church. Ed.
Norbert Greinacher and Alois
Müller. 0 8164 2147 1 128pp.
Christianity and Socialism. Ed.
Johannes Baptist Metz and Jean-
Pierre Jossua. 0 8164 2148 X
144pp.
The Churches of Africa: Future
Prospects. Ed. Claude Geffré and
Bertrand Luneau. 0 8164 2150 1
128pp.
Judgement in the Church. Ed.
William Bassett and Peter
Huizing. 0 8164 2166 8 128pp.
Why Did God Make Me? Ed.
Hans Küng and Jürgen
Moltmann. 0 8164 2167 6 112pp.
Charisms in the Church. Ed.
Christian Duquoc and Casiano
Floristán. 0 8164 2168 4 128pp.
Moral Formation and Christianity.
Ed. Franz Bockle and Jacques
Marie Pohier. 0 8164 2169 2
90pp.
Communication in the Church. Ed.
Gregory Baum and Andrew
Greeley. 0 8164 2170 6 126pp.

112. **Liturgy and Human Passage.** Ed.
David Power and Luis
Maldonado. 0 8164 2608 2 136pp.
113. **Revelation and Experience.** Ed.
Edward Schillebeeckx and Bas
van Iersel. 0 8164 2609 0 134pp.
114. **Evangelization in the World
Today.** Ed. Norbert Greinacher
and Alois Müller. 0 8164 2610 4
136pp.
115. **Doing Theology in New Places.**
Ed. Jean-Pierre Jossua and
Johannes Baptist Metz.
0 8164 2611 2 120pp.
116. **Buddhism and Christianity.** Ed.
Claude Geffré and Mariasusai
Dhavamony. 0 8164 2612 0 136pp.
117. **The Finances of the Church.** Ed.
William Bassett and Peter
Huizing. 0 8164 2197 8 160pp.
118. **An Ecumenical Confession of
Faith?** Ed. Hans Küng and Jürgen
Moltmann. 0 8164 2198 6 136pp.
119. **Discernment of the Spirit and of
Spirits.** Ed. Casiano Floristán and
Christian Duquoc. 0 8164 2199 4
136pp.
120. **The Death Penalty and Torture.**
Ed. Franz Bockle and Jacques
Marie Pohier. 0 8164 2200 1
136pp.
121. **The Family in Crisis or in
Transition.** Ed. Andrew Greeley.
0 567 30001 3 128pp.
122. **Structures of Initiation in Crisis.**
Ed. Luis Maldonado and David
Power. 0 567 30002 1 128pp.
123. **Heaven.** Ed. Bas van Iersel and
Edward Schillebeeckx.
0 567 30003 X 120pp.
124. **The Church and the Rights of
Man.** Ed. Alois Müller and
Norbert Greinacher. 0 567 30004 8
140pp.
125. **Christianity and the Bourgeoisie.**
Ed. Johannes Baptist Metz.
0 567 30005 6 144pp.
126. **China as a Challenge to the
Church.** Ed. Claude Geffré and
Joseph Spae. 0 567 30006 4 136pp.
127. **The Roman Curia and the
Communion of Churches.** Ed.
Peter Huizing and Knut Walf.
0 567 30007 2 144pp.
128. **Conflicts about the Holy Spirit.**
Ed. Hans Küng and Jürgen
Moltmann. 0 567 30008 0 144pp.
129. **Models of Holiness.** Ed. Christian
Duquoc and Casiano Floristán.
0 567 30009 9 128pp.
130. **The Dignity of the Despised of the
Earth.** Ed. Jacques Marie Pohier
and Dietmar Mieth. 0 567 30010 2
144pp.
131. **Work and Religion.** Ed. Gregory
Baum. 0 567 30011 0 148pp.
132. **Symbol and Art in Worship.** Ed.
Luis Maldonado and David
Power. 0 567 30012 9 136pp.
133. **Right of the Community to a
Priest.** Ed. Edward Schillebeeckx
and Johannes Baptist Metz.
0 567 30013 7 148pp.
134. **Women in a Men's Church.** Ed.
Virgil Elizondo and Norbert
Greinacher. 0 567 30014 5 144pp.
135. **True and False Universality of
Christianity.** Ed. Claude Geffré
and Jean-Pierre Jossua.
0 567 30015 3 138pp.

136. **What is Religion? An Inquiry for
Christian Theology.** Ed. Mircea
Eliade and David Tracy.
0 567 30016 1 98pp.
137. **Electing our Own Bishops.** Ed.
Peter Huizing and Knut Walf.
0 567 30017 X 112pp.
138. **Conflicting Ways of Interpreting
the Bible.** Ed. Hans Küng and
Jürgen Moltmann. 0 567 30018 8
112pp.
139. **Christian Obedience.** Ed. Casiano
Floristán and Christian Duquoc.
0 567 30019 6 96pp.
140. **Christian Ethics and Economics:
the North-South Conflict.** Ed.
Dietmar Mieth and Jacques Marie
Pohier. 0 567 30020 X 128pp.
141. **Neo-Conservatism: Social and
Religious Phenomenon.** Ed.
Gregory Baum and John
Coleman. 0 567 30021 8.
142. **The Times of Celebration.** Ed.
David Power and Mary Collins.
0 567 30022 6.
143. **God as Father.** Ed. Edward
Schillebeeckx and Johannes
Baptist Metz. 0 567 30023 4.
144. **Tensions Between the Churches of
the First World and the Third
World.** Ed. Virgil Elizondo and
Norbert Greinacher.
0 567 30024 2.
145. **Nietzsche and Christianity.** Ed.
Claude Geffré and Jean-Pierre
Jossua. 0 567 30025 0.
146. **Where Does the Church Stand?**
Ed. Giuseppe Alberigo.
0 567 30026 9.
147. **The Revised Code of Canon Law:
a Missed Opportunity?** Ed. Peter
Huizing and Knut Walf.
0 567 30027 7.
148. **Who Has the Say in the Church?**
Ed. Hans Küng and Jürgen
Moltmann. 0 567 30028 5.
149. **Francis of Assisi Today.** Ed.
Casiano Floristán and Christian
Duquoc. 0 567 30029 3.
150. **Christian Ethics: Uniformity,
Universality, Pluralism.** Ed.
Jacques Pohier and Dietmar
Mieth. 0 567 30030 7.
151. **The Church and Racism.** Ed.
Gregory Baum and John
Coleman. 0 567 30031 5.
152. **Can we always celebrate the
Eucharist?** Ed. Mary Collins and
David Power. 0 567 30032 3.
153. **Jesus, Son of God?** Ed. Edward
Schillebeeckx and Johannes-
Baptist Metz. 0 567 30033 1.
154. **Religion and Churches in Eastern
Europe.** Ed. Virgil ELizondo and
Norbert Greinacher.
0 567 30034 X.
155. **'The Human', Criterion of
Christian Existence?** Ed. Claude
Geffré and Jean-Pierre Jossua.
0 567 30035 8.
156. **The Challenge of Psychology to
Faith.** Ed. Steven Kepnes (Guest
Editor) and David Tracy.
0 567 30036 6.
157. **May Church Ministers be
Politicians?** Ed. Peter Huizing and
Knut Walf. 0 567 30037 4.
158. **The Right to Dissent.** Ed. Hans
Küng and Jürgen Moltmann.
0 567 30038 2.

CONCILIUM

CONCILIUM 1987

All back issues are still in print: available from bookshops (price £5.45) or direct from the publishers (£5.95/US$9.95/Can$11.75 including postage and packing).

T & T CLARK LTD, 59 GEORGE STREET, EDINBURGH EH2 2LQ, SCOTLAND